# WHAT PEOPL[E]
# SAID ABOUT

'I know it's a cliché, but you are worth you weight in gold.'
*Researcher, University of Sydney*

'The informal feedback has been outstanding and
I think you have helped us immensely.'
*Institute Director, La Trobe University*

'The LinkedIn Masterclass on Research Translation facilitated
by Jane Anderson and Dr Richard Huysmans was superb.
Highly recommend this to all Australian Researchers looking
to research out to the world.'
*A/Prof and Platform Manager, La Trobe University*

'Thanks for your advice Richard, it gave me a totally new
perspective on my PhD and work possibilities.'
*PhD Student, Monash Health*

'Thanks a lot for your message. A lot of good advice there.'
*Researcher, Institute Curie*

'Richard is easy to talk to and he enabled me to actively find
solutions to move me forward in a positive way. I would have no
hesitations whatsoever in recommending Richard to anyone who's
keen to change career paths, in particular from an academic career
into industry. I always enjoy catching up with Richard.'
*[Former] Researcher, Monash University*

'Richard Huysmans is an Owl (Older, Wise Learner). He has a great
knack at identifying transferable skills and helping you think outside
the box for job prospects.'
*Ruth Wagstaff, PhD Student*

CONNECT THE DOCS

# CONNECT THE DOCS:

## A GUIDE TO GETTING INDUSTRY PARTNERS, AS AN ACADEMIC

DR RICHARD HUYSMANS

First Published in 2019 by Baker Street Press | Melbourne

ISBN 9780648281221

A catalogue record of this book is available from the
National Library of Australia

Edited by Joanna Yardley at The Editing House

Cover design and typeset by Jane Radman at JRadman Design

# TABLE OF CONTENTS

# INTRODUCTION

In my experience with helping researchers engage other researchers, potential industry partners or end users, I have never met a researcher who is fond of selling. In fact, I would go as far as to say all researchers based at universities see their role as explicitly avoiding selling, particularly avoiding selling their ideas to end users for commercial gain.

However, the same researchers are very keen on positioning themselves for the best possible collaborative and grant-related research opportunities. This is the key to overcoming apprehension when it comes to end-user engagement or the translation of research outcomes into everyday use. The academic approach is the key to responding to the challenges you face, but it needs to be applied outside academia.

Researchers need to shift their focus from selling to positioning. Rather than trying to sell themselves, their work or their findings, they should focus on positioning. Instead of telling people how good you are at data analysis, write an article about data analysis. Instead of telling people how good you are at survey development, share examples of excellent surveys. Instead of telling people how good you are at discovering cell-signalling pathways, comment on the quality of other people's work.

Essentially, get known as the expert by people, organisations, industries or sectors who might be interested in your work. It is about doing the work that shows you as the expert, rather than just being the expert nobody knows.

# PART ONE:
## THE RESEARCH GAME

# CHAPTER 1

# WHAT A RESEARCHER WANTS

In late 2014, #IAmAScientistBecause started on Twitter. @PrincessSuperno tweeted '#IAmAScientistBecause what's more awesome than working out how supernovae explode? #CCSN #physics'.[1]

The movement did not make a real impact until April 2015, when researchers took to Twitter to describe—in less than 140 characters—why they were researchers.[2] People have approached this in many ways: videos, pictures, photos, links, research and, of course, just a few words. It has since become more popular with photo booths springing up at various careers expos and conferences highlighting #IAmAScientistBecause. As such, events continue to focus on the hashtag and it has become a trending hashtag among researchers.

Looking through the stream of hashtags, the reasons for becoming a scientist can be categorised into one or more themes:

- They are inspired into research.
- They are out to make a difference.
- They are curious about the world.
- They want to be at the cutting edge of knowledge.
- They are out to work on projects they want, with people they like, in places they love.

When I talk and work with researchers, these reasons are often the reasons they cite for becoming researchers and continuing to do research. Of course, in many cases there is a blend of one or more reasons.

What is clear and absent is that unlike other career paths, no one chooses research to:

- Make money
- Have a secure future
- Sell ideas to others.

Similarly, being a researcher is not a destination career like a lawyer, an accountant or a teacher. Once you qualify as a researcher, you still face a life-long, self-directed path to learning and discovery—the process we call research.

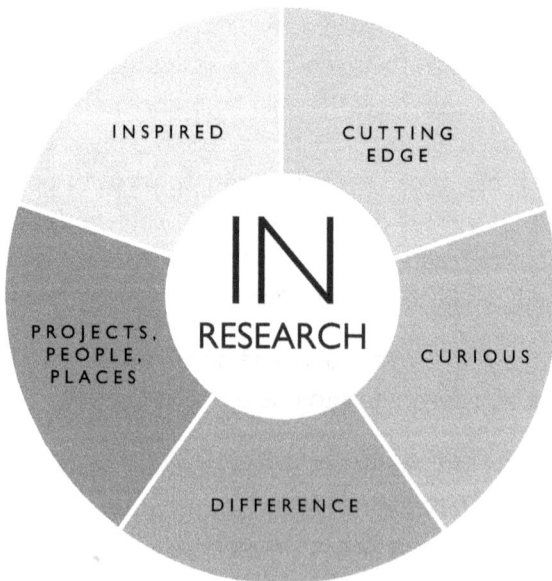

**FIGURE I:** WHY PEOPLE BECOME RESEARCHERS

## TO BE INSPIRED

You can tell, almost immediately, when someone has been inspired into research. It comes out in everything they do and say. Much like an artist, each piece of work has its own story guiding the development of the work. However, in the case of researchers, experiments, grant applications and journal articles have the own stories.

Sources of inspiration can vary. For some it is an early childhood experience. For others, it is the emotion of witnessing a family member go through cancer or seeing injustice in the world that needs to be fixed. Then of course, there are people who had teachers who inspired them through their action. Such teachers often influence students in their high school years, but can also inspire students earlier in their primary years, or later in their tertiary years.

As a PhD candidate in a biomedical science laboratory focused on cell signalling, many of my colleagues were in this category. That is, they were inspired into research through personal experience. Indeed, some sought out the laboratory because the signalling pathways and associated proteins and molecules being investigated were implicated in the cancer or diseases in which they were interested.

### PROBLEM

The problem with being driven by inspiration or inspired into research is that when inspiration leaves you, research can be hard. A bit like when writer's block prevents authors from achieving their goals, people inspired into research struggle with research if inspiration leaves them. Their motivation can drop and as a result, their research outputs such as grants and peer-reviewed papers can drop. Over a prolonged period, this can lead to productivity gaps that can be hard to explain away. It can also lead to crises of confidence and a feeling of needing or wanting to leave research.

## SOLUTION

The solution is to maintain an inspiration folder. This is a paper or electronic folder that contains pictures, articles, words, notes or emails that have affirmed your inspiration. It's not a list of inspirational quotes, rather a list of quotes from people you know who inspire or encourage you to keep working.

It may also be the case that inspiration has actually left you. Acknowledging this fact will be key to reinvigorating your career in research or changing direction and moving into something else.

# TO MAKE A DIFFERENCE

Closely related to being inspired into research (and perhaps overlapping it) is joining research in order to make a difference. This tends to be strong driver for people in health, medical and social research. Of course, those fields also have front line workers separate from researchers. In many cases, those in research have determined that their best/biggest impact can be made by undertaking research rather than being a front line worker.

The desire to make a difference through research can also come from direct life experiences such as health problems or social issues. However, there is definitely a large group of researchers who can do many things well, but feel they can impact the world most effectively by being researchers whose work is translated into practice or cures.

This is the case for a professor with whom I work. As a trained social worker, she felt the biggest difference she could make to the lives of people with disabilities was not be to a front-line social worker. Rather, it was all about researching the best ways to support people with a disability and ensure those methods were implemented across the disability sectors (national and international). Consistent with this approach, she works closely with disability service providers, as well as state and federal governments. In terms of making a difference, the research findings can be put into practice at the coalface and/or turned into policy directives.

In some respects, you could liken this reason as a calling into research. In the same way that many religious leaders describe being called into their role, these researchers are clear that their best career, the one that they will make the biggest positive impact on the world, is in research.

### PROBLEM

Those who are in research to make a difference are often driven by seeing the impact of their work. They like to see organisations, industries, sectors and governments implement their work. The larger the impact, the better. However, when you are so connected to your work, if it is not implemented or implemented poorly, it can be difficult to keep going.

### SOLUTION

If you are in research to make a difference, it is important to recognise that 'no' may actually mean 'not now'. A follow-up email or call, at a later date, might be met with a different answer. It is also worth bearing in mind that change and influencing change can happen at many levels—within an individual department all the way through to policy. So, if you fail at the policy level, try at the department level (and vice versa).

## CONSTANTLY CURIOUS

Most researchers are innately curious, but not all are drawn to research because of this curiosity. Curiosity is definitely a driver for most (if not all) researchers, but it is not always the reason they became a researcher in the first place. For some, curiosity strikes them early in life—at school or during their degree training. For others, it comes later during honours or masters or even within their PhD. Regardless, it is a strong driver of research life.

For lots of researchers driven by curiosity, it is a case of nothing ventured nothing gained. In many respects, it is a high-risk, high-reward approach to research. For them, conducting research is not just a chance to answer a question; it is a chance to answer a question so more can be posed. These researchers never lost their inner 2-year-old self and are always asking why.

I know a professor of physics who became a researcher for just this reason. His early worked focused on magnetic resonance imaging, and it has never really changed. As the field moved forward, so did he. Thirty years on, he is still solving problems of imaging; problems identified as a result of his early research.

## PROBLEM

Researchers driven by curiosity can have research expertise that spans too many fields or disciplines. Constantly asking why means they can move on to a new field in search of more questions to answer, rather than progressing through to the logical end of a piece of work. They can also get caught in the semantics of applied versus fundamental research.

## SOLUTION

Creating a plan or pathway towards an outcome can help keep curiosity-driven researchers moving in the same direction. Of course, it is important to refer regularly back to the plan to ensure you have not deviated from it, or if you have, that it is justifiable. When a curious researcher collaborates with a researcher who is driven to make a difference, a perfect partnership that matches thinking with action is created.

## AT THE CUTTING EDGE

Until a researcher's work is published, it is only you and your collaborators who know that thing. In my case, it was a communication pathway within specific cells. For other biomedical researchers, it can be the crystal or 3D structure of a protein or group of proteins. And for social researchers, it can be the leadership or cultural structures that are the keys to success (or failure) in an organisation or situation.

This was my driving force for getting into research. Even when I think about it now, it was being at the cutting edge of knowledge that thrilled me most about my PhD. And all other life factors being equal, it is potentially the one thing that could entice me back. [3]

People driven by the idea of being not just at the cutting edge, but the bleeding edge are at the forefront of the innovation adoption lifecycle (see figure 2). They are the innovators bringing the new ideas into the main stream; they are the people who line up for the latest phone, computer, car or solar electricity system.

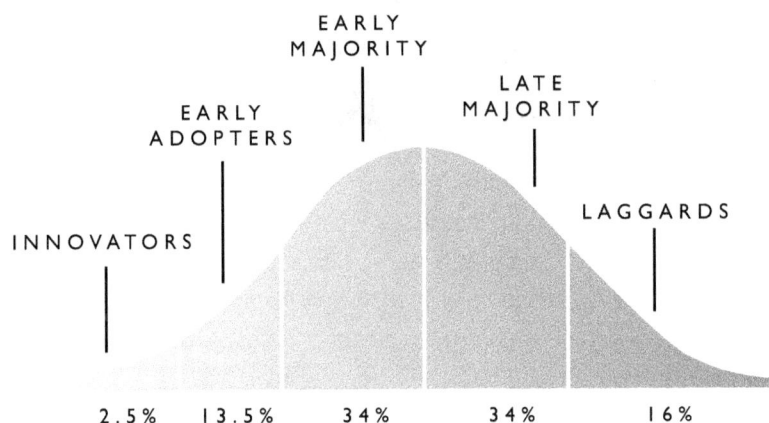

**FIGURE 2:** INNOVATION ADOPTION LIFESTYLE[4]

## PROBLEM

If you are driven by being at the cutting edge then getting scooped can hurt ... really hurt. Not just because your research is no longer publishable at the same level or with the same impact, but because you are no longer the only person with that knowledge. Of course, being scooped is a problem for all researchers. Being at the cutting edge can also mean that very few people care about the work in the way that you do. In an interview on ABC Radio, Professor Peter Doherty noted (and I am paraphrasing) *You are simultaneously one of a few people in the world who know something and also among a similarly small group of people who care about that thing.*[5] This can make it hard to translate your work into outcomes with impact beyond your own research world let alone someone else's research world or society as a whole.

## SOLUTION

In one respect, the solution is to publish more often or sooner. I know of researchers who will design a piece of work with the end publication in mind—the journal, the topic, the figures and the authors. This makes it easier for them to know when they are ready to publish as well as to know the level of evidence and kinds of data they would need in order to pass the peer review process. Of course, this is easier said than done, and their career stage needs to be taken into account.

There is some evidence to suggest publishing earlier is more important than publishing in high impact factor journals as a predictor of overall research career success.[6] As a person driven by curiosity, it is worth trying to find someone driven by being at the cutting edge and collaborating with people who are driven by a desire to have an impact.

# PERFECT PROJECTS, PEOPLE, AND PLACES

As a researcher, you get to choose whom you work with, particularly if you are the head of a research group. You get to hire or recruit all of the workers, approve all of applications for PhD projects, and make a major contribution to all of the grants. Your research topic is generally one of the biggest interests in your life. You might even do the work for free if your financial situation allowed it. [7]

Perfect projects are all about the research methodology. As the saying goes, 'there are many ways to skin a cat' and in research, there are likely many research methods that will help a researcher arrive at a suitable solution to a problem.

Perfect places refer to inside or outside, lab or office, field or forest. Many researchers have chosen their topic of interest because it includes the right combination of places. Of course, as the nature of work has shifted, it has allowed researchers to shift their location too—many traditional offices have been replaced by work-from-home scenarios.

Perfect people cover a range of factors from personalities to thought processes to quickness of thinking to views on the world. This is not to say researchers do not have differing views on the world or major arguments—on the contrary. However, the ability to choose whom you work with means these kinds of differences are not present in the same research group. The competitive nature of research funding ensures differences exist across the sector and within specialities as a whole.

## PROBLEM

The problem with being attracted to research for the perfect projects, places and/or people means you can be willing to work for free. You love your work so much that you put in extra time. This extra time often goes towards improving your career or standing in research. However, if that relationship is not linear—or close to linear—it can get disheartening to work ever harder for what seems like—and could actually be—no result. Indeed, in a talk on ABC Radio in 2016, Nobel Laureate Professor Peter Doherty noted that excellent research includes a fair degree of good luck choosing the right research question and/or research methodology.

## SOLUTION

Every now and again, it pays to listen to the feedback, advice or concerns of friends, family and even other researchers who can see you working harder and perhaps neglecting other parts of your life. A bit like people who keep an exercise diary, consider keeping a logbook of your hours worked. Reviewing your work diary will help you identify times, places and circumstances where you are more likely to work too hard or too long.

# CHAPTER 2

# CONDUCTING RESEARCH
# IS HARD

At this point, if you are under the impression that research is easy, let me say now that it is not. It is hard. Even if you are only worried about your work, many things need to come together for success to happen.

Consider the process of becoming qualified as a researcher. First, you need to go to university. Roughly 50 percent of high school graduates go to university, and 80 percent of those will pass. About 30 percent will then go on to study a PhD. Only 50 percent of that 30 percent will start an academic research career. But only 2–5 percent stay in research for a further ten years or more. So, if we started with 1,000 high school graduates:

- 500 will go to university (3–5 years)
- 400 will graduate their degree
- 120 will do further study such as a PhD (3–5 years, but many will be 7 years or more)
- 60 will start an academic career (3–5 years for your first post-doctoral research position)[8]
- 1–2 will remain in research for 10 years or more.

If nothing else, you at least need persistence in order to become a researcher, and even more persistence to be successful. However, you need to be hardworking and extremely lucky to choose a problem that ends up needing a captivating solution. Indeed, Professor Peter Doherty said the same in relation to his Nobel Prize.

In many respects, being an academic can be likened to being a high-performing Olympic athlete in an obscure sport. Of course, the process is long, but the foundations are the same—hard work over a long period of time leads to success. In small Olympic sports, you work all of your life to get to the pinnacle of your career, putting in lots of extra time and your own funds, to have the opportunity to be in the public spotlight once in four years.

## THE MOVING PARTS OF RESEARCH SUCCESS

Becoming a successful researcher is more than progressing through a series of education steps. For example, completing a degree and a PhD does not make you a researcher; however, both are essential. Once you have completed your PhD, there are many moving parts that you continue to hone at the production end.

There are four factors (moving parts) that influence research success.

- Choose a **topic**: the focus of your research or what you avoid becoming part of your research.
- Decide on a research **method**: the approaches you use to investigate your topic of interest.
- Obtain the best **infrastructure**: the equipment and facilities you use (or require) to implement your chosen methodological approach(es) in the context of your research topic.
- Recruit good **people**: staff, students and collaborators that form the various teams involved in the delivery of an outcome.

Finally, you have to hope it all comes together at the same time to ensure the maximum chance of success. Of course, this is all in the context of writing grants and publishing your research.

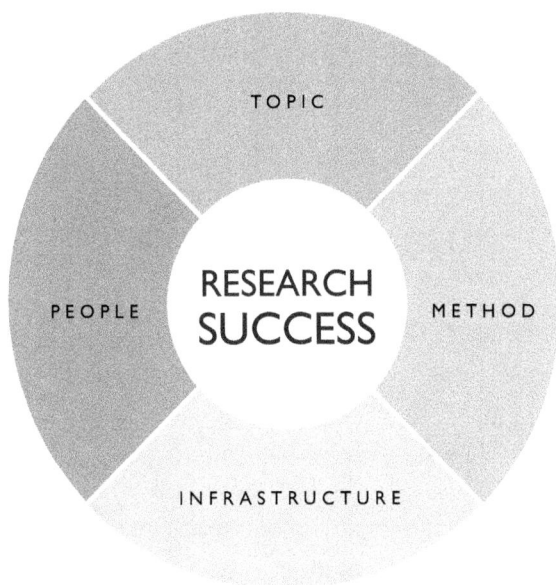

**FIGURE 3:** THE MOVING PARTS OF RESEARCH SUCCESS

## TOPIC

Research topic is all about your research focus. For many, this was actually set at the time of embarking on your PhD. For others it means your research topic fell into a broad area of interest (e.g. biochemistry) or the topic was a very deliberate choice (e.g. helping people deal with death through art). Regardless, if you have continued into a research career, even if it is part time, you likely continued following the same research path (topic) of your PhD. It is clearly not a bad thing for your research career to follow on from your PhD. However, it is worth considering the impact of your topic choice on your research success to date as well as the future.

For some, there are many ways to express your topic of interest, and it may change depending on the audience. It is accepted that researchers review and subsequently refine their research topic based on grant guidelines, funding organisation priorities or previous research/grant/funding success. For example, a researcher with a focus on osteoarthritis of the knee could describe their topic of interest as one or more of the following:

- Knee anatomy
- Arthritis
- Osteoarthritis
- Chronic disease
- Ageing
- Sport
- Sports injuries
- Over-use injuries.

There are probably many other options as well; therefore, it is important to understand how your topic might fit with the focus of the day.

I noted earlier that people come to research for various reasons and several include a relationship to the research topic. For example, Inspiration, Difference and Curiosity all have large components of topic already attached to them. This may mean you feel your research topic is a little less flexible; that you do not have the opportunity to change it if the funding landscape changes or if new, relevant but nonetheless different, opportunities present themselves.

For example, research into issues of ageing has not always been popular. In the 1980s and 1990s, the tsunami of older people due to leave the workforce and the relative wading pool size of the population entering the workforce were not envisaged. Many researchers in the field of ageing struggled to obtain support for proposals where ageing was the sole or major focus. During those times, it could be argued their research suffered, and they were less successful than they might have been had they changed their topic. However, since the 2000s, issues of ageing across social, environmental and health fields have come to prominence, and many researchers try to relate their topic to ageing even if the link is tenuous. This is not to say it is easy being a researcher with a focus on ageing. There are many researchers, with a focus on ageing, who comment on the relative bias towards Alzheimer's disease particularly at the expense of other neurological diseases of ageing such as Parkinson's disease and other dementias.

It is also clear that assessments such as the Excellence in Research for Australia (ERA) exercise and the Research Excellence Framework in the UK are encouraging people to reconsider how their research is defined or described. In these assessments, those you work with or avoid can impact how your research is ranked in relation to your peers, within and outside of your organisation. Such refinements might give your research a competitive advantage.

Regardless, clear choice of research topic adds to the complexity of research success. However, even being open to changing topic can lead to portfolio careers, where a researcher might be viewed as not being sufficiently experienced or expert in a field in order to be deemed competitive.

## METHOD

Is there method to your madness or madness in your method? We all know that you need to design the research correctly; this includes choosing the right method. However, whether we like it or not, some methods are more right than others. If you have been in research for a continuous period, you would be aware of these shifts. A simple example might be transitioning away from research involving animals to other forms of research where animals are not involved.

Some complex examples might be the greater use of technology to achieve research outcomes. For example, the use of eye scanning and facial recognition software to determine the impact of certain advertising campaigns on a population or the use of electronic and, now, mobile-phone-based surveys rather than paper-based surveys.

Of course, not all technological advances should be taken as and when they arrive. For the 2016 Australian Census, organisers transitioned to an online only approach or paper by exception. They spooked the entire population regarding data retention, data security and privacy. Ultimately, the response rate was only slightly lower than previous censuses, but the Australian population became sceptical of the government's ability to operate a national survey electronically.

So, although there might be many ways to bake a cake you must have the end point in mind when determining the method: Do you want one cake or several? Do people have allergies? Do you have flavour or colour preferences? What is the occasion?

In the same way, these types of questions all impact research methodology. Inadvertently using one method over another may dramatically impact the outcome. Going back to our Australian Census example, there are many researchers and commentators who feel the online approach negatively impacted the quality of responses received. Certainly, the response rate was impacted in the early weeks following the census date. However, at its conclusion the census was broadly reported as having met its response target—94.4 percent of households responded versus a target of 95 percent. However, concerns were raised about the quality of responses and if the data can be trusted.

Other examples of methodological selections impacting outcomes often focus on animal research, whereby use of the right or wrong animal during a trial can lead to outcomes that do not translate well to human use. Thalidomide had difficulty replicating the human effects in animals. Conversely, aspartame, despite effects seen in animals, could not be replicated in humans.

Of course, many factors impact methodological choice besides desired end result. In both the examples above, cost was a major factor. In the Australian Census, transition to an electronic version was fast-tracked to keep costs down. The 2011 census had both options with paper the default option. In that instance, 30 percent completed the online version. In 2016, the target was 65 percent using online, but only 59 precent participated.

Similarly, it may be possible to find the animal that mimics human physiology closest. However, over years of research, we have established that for different biological pathways or physiological responses, different animals are better human analogues than others, and it is unrealistic to test them all. Indeed, this is often used as an argument to stop research using animals.

For a researcher, money might mean the difference between a pilot or small-scale study and a full-blown piece of research. Although pilot or small-scale studies are meant to have a similar outcome to their larger counterparts, they are structurally limited. They are only able to find large effect sizes. Therefore, small but significant findings are harder to identify in small-scale trials and pilot studies.

As a researcher, your choice of methodology is paramount to your research success, and sometimes that can be difficult to predict or select in advance.

## INFRASTRUCTURE

The infrastructure, to which you have access, is a result of many factors. These include the organisation you are part of, the state or country it is in, and your field of research. Some would also argue that your research standing—in all of those areas—also impacts your access to that equipment.

As a researcher, you have some control over this. You can choose your field; you can seek employment at your preferred institute (but that is not always how it works out); and you can write grants for equipment. However, a large amount of infrastructure is largely out of your control. Take, for example, how you might access research infrastructure that is at the mid-tier. Not the kind of equipment that is now considered National Collaborative Research Infrastructure in Australia, but elements provided by your employer. These could include IT, data storage, office space, and research lab space. People or entities outside the sphere of influence of the average researcher control most of these elements.

Even if you do manage to secure some of your own equipment, on-going operation and maintenance is beyond what an individual researcher or research group might be able to afford, particularly if your use of the equipment is relatively low, say 30 percent or less than the available operational time. Similarly, access to specific cohorts of participants can also be problematic. Certain universities have, what amounts to, exclusive relationships with service providers limiting access to researchers from other institutions. As a result, sometimes you have to make do with what is available. That can mean the equivalent of trying to kill a fly with a sledgehammer. Although it is effective, it means you spend far more time, effort and money than is necessary, and you perfect the technique with sub-optimal or over-engineered equipment or you retrospectively justify why the choice was perfect for your research question.

At other times, you might be lucky enough to secure the perfect piece of equipment for the job, but fail to attract the necessary support infrastructure. It could be argued this has happened within the biomedical imaging field—in particular, molecular imaging. Purchase of the equipment is lengthy and requires collaboration across multiple institutions. Subsequent use of the equipment requires radioactive materials. Safe and consistent generation of these materials takes place in purpose built and designed facilities.

Many applicants argue this can be solved with existing equipment. That is certainly true, but cutting edge tracers (as these radioactive materials are referred to) are often special and their radioactivity is short lived. This is great—it reduces radiation exposure to the participant—but it means transport is difficult. Anything farther than a couple of hours away from the production facility, can render the imaging facility somewhat useless for development and testing of new tracers.

These factors, combined with the reality that much research infrastructure is fixed or only obtainable through grants, means that success as a researcher shifts further out of your direct control.

## PEOPLE

Modern research is highly collaborative. Although the data on Nobel Prize winners suggests they are less collaborative and produce more single author papers than their non-prize winning counterparts,[9] the reality is it is impossible to succeed in research (in Australia) without collaboration.

For most researchers, success also requires building a larger research team or group; much like a small business grows its staff in order to increase its capability and capacity to deliver products or services. Added to this, researchers are required to supervise students. This increases the number of people you must work with as a researcher. Therefore, working with others is an essential part of research success.

Of course, we do not (or perhaps cannot) get along well with all people, all of the time. Furthermore, in a collaborative arrangement with a student or an experienced researcher, there are times when the work we do depends on the work of others. For example, we work in series rather than in parallel. This means our success is linked to the work ethic and success of our collaborators. Although we do our best to ensure we can work with the people we choose as collaborators, things do not always operate smoothly. Even if two people get along well, it is difficult, perhaps impossible, to predict if the research will proceed as planned. Indeed, if research did proceed as planned, the world would be a boring place where all of our hypotheses are accepted and everything is known.

The opposite may also be true where your collaborators are waiting on your work for their success.

Of course, there may also be times where you wish you could get access to a particular collaborator or student, but they are beyond your reach. Perhaps you struggle to arrange a meeting time or they are busy overseas or they get attracted to another research team. It's a bit like parking at the supermarket, all of the good spaces get taken first. Or perhaps it's more like surge pricing for Uber: certain events drive demand for specific services that then become more expensive to access.

When it comes to people, recruitment is only the start of the problem. Once you have attracted them, it is a constant struggle to retain them. Have you enough money? Have you enough work? Is the work interesting? Are they developing as a researcher?

Then, if they leave the cycle starts all over again. Thus, success as a researcher relies on attracting and retaining great staff, students and collaborators—but great people are sometimes elusive.

## NOISE, NUISANCE OR NOTICED

A mentor of mine, Matt Church, often says, 'you don't matter, they're not listening, and no one cares'. Ironically, its meant to inspire confidence to write and put work into the public domain. Somehow it works. It gets me over my concerns that what I write might be misconstrued. I'm afraid of offending someone, rather than worried about being noticed. As a consultant, not being noticed has a greater impact than offending someone. For the most part, the same is true for researchers. Generally, it is better to publish and be noticed or criticised than not to publish and never be criticised.

For many researchers, being noticed is a bit like *Where's Wally?* The scenery and other characters all look similar making it almost impossible to find Wally no matter how hard you look. Then, when you think you've found Wally, it really isn't him. There's one feature missing, or not quite right. In research, it can feel like there is always something missing or not quite right when it comes to putting your research out there.

In 2016, an ad ran on Australian TV featuring a child mimicking their dad driving a car. The child repeated the dad's words, 'bloody caravaners'. The ad received just over 150 complaints. At about the same time, an ad aired for a website encouraging discrete relationships. It received 120 complaints. Presuming about 10 million people watch TV in Australia and 5 million could make a complaint, it means less than 0.00004 percent of people were listening, felt the ad mattered, and cared enough to complain. It also shows that 'bloody' said by a child is more offensive than encouraging infidelity.

As a researcher, it feels like no one is listening. Ever. Unless, of course, they are a reviewer, in which case they find everything wrong with your grant application or journal article. They are the 0.000004 percent. It can be hard to work day in, day out on something that apparently no one cares for, is listening to or sees as relevant to them. Therein lies the problem: we're more in danger of being invisible than being offensive. Yet we are driven by concern over being offensive.

Of course, when it comes to being noticed, fear of being controversial is not the first (or only) problem. For most researchers, their position in their organisation is buried. Buried beneath a department, perhaps a school, a faculty, a college and then a university.

To move up the layers—or perhaps get rid of them all together—researchers often form groups, centres or institutes (see figure 4). Those sceptical of such moves often equate them to rearranging the deck chairs on the Titanic. For some researchers, these can be positive moves as they generate a new impetus for working with new or different collaborators. For others, rearranging the deck chairs on the Titanic is probably an apt description.

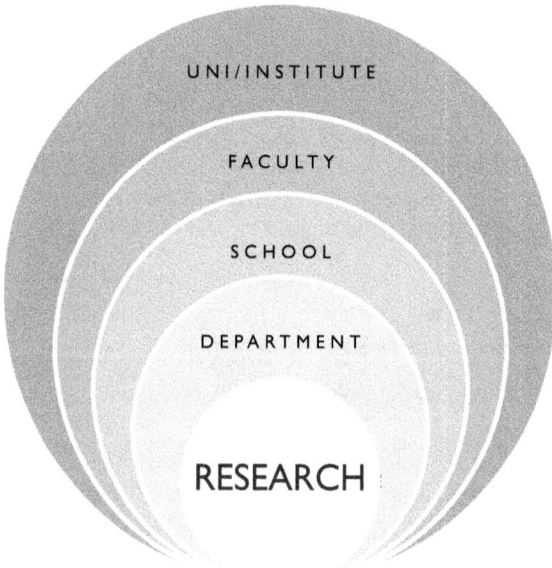

**FIGURE 4:** WHERE RESEARCHERS ARE POSITIONED IN THEIR ORGANISATION

For researchers, success is littered with examples of failure. Consider Charles Darwin and his theory of evolution; it was first proposed in 1859 but not completely accepted (or noticed) as a theory until the 1930s.

In 2012, Professor Colin Raston and colleagues from the University of Adelaide embarked on research that essentially allowed them to unboil an egg. [10] Of course, that's not the sole purpose of the work. It has useful applications in drug delivery and is already being used in cancer drug development. Nonetheless, they were awarded an Ig Noble Prize for their work. This perhaps confined the research to something to laugh about and ask 'did we actually spend tax payer dollars on that?'

On many levels, the egg research was successful in terms of getting noticed. And I am sure the researchers and universities involved chose to promote the research in the context of unboiling an egg, rather than improving drug production for cancer treatment.

Ultimately, researchers sometimes feel that getting noticed is a choice between being noisy and being a nuisance. In reality, it needs to be more like search engine optimisation, where you create an environment that facilitates being found, rather than shouting, 'look at me' all of the time. However, in order to be found you at least need to be in the public domain.

# CHAPTER 3

# PUBLISH OR PERISH

Publishing research is difficult. Yet, we operate in an academic world where the mantra is publish or perish. That says it all. If your research work is not published, your research career comes to a grinding halt. A bit like playing sport, it starts out as fun and ends up being all about the games won and lost. You start out in gymnastics or soccer because it is fun to do. There is no difference between training and competition. But the longer you stay in gymnastics or soccer, the less training and competition look the same. Training is often a chore, and you pine for the competition.

It's the same in research. You undertook your PhD to make a difference, contribute knowledge to the world, or work at the cutting edge of science. Work that progresses the knowledge base is no different to work that might contribute to a research paper. However, the further you move into your research career, progressing from honours to PhD and to an early career researcher, the more you focus on scores, and winning and losing. Then you focus more on the publishability of the work and not on making a difference, contributing knowledge or working at the cutting edge.

Over the years, almost without exception, I have not met a researcher who does not have a drawer full of partially started, partially finished or submitted and rejected journal articles. Each has its own unique story within the research and pertaining to the writing process itself. All of them have, for some reason, stalled. Sometimes a collaborator left the collaboration, the university, the country or the sector altogether. Other times that final experiment just never worked. Controls fail, participants are not quite right or, worse still, you cannot replicate the work of others. Then, if you bring it all together into an article and submit it for review, you have to deal with reviewer comments— either rebutting them or agreeing—which results in more work. In the meantime, the field, grant or opportunity has somehow moved on and your motivation for completing the paper is not there. You're focused on a new research direction and that's okay, and so the paper gets added to the 'almost complete' list.

## THE MOVING PARTS OF PUBLISH OR PERISH

Of course getting a piece of research published, as a peer-reviewed journal article, is not a trivial task. There are many moving parts. Most are, at best, choices we have to make and, at worse, out of our control.

PERISH

RESEARCH

WRITE

JOURNAL
SELECTION

REVIEW

PUBLISH

**FIGURE 5:** THE MOVING PARTS BETWEEN PERISH AND PUBLISH

## RESEARCH

The first moving part is the research itself. Conducting research is not easy, but it is largely in your control. As a PhD student, I saw this part as an exercise in determination. Those who were determined enough progressed their intended research. This does not mean determination equates with completed research. Indeed, just because you completed the research does not mean it was a success. You might have findings that you struggle to replicate. The work might refute existing theories or literature. Worse still, you might try repeatedly but fail to reproduce some previously published work, preventing progress to the stage where your expertise would add value.

## WRITING

The next moving part is the writing. Writing a journal article is a bit like running a marathon. No matter how hard you train, no matter how many times you have done it before, it is still tough. And, to mix metaphors, it's a bit like bringing up children—the process for writing is not the same for any two journal articles.

As part of the writing process, you need to select the journal, and there are many factors to consider here:

- Review processes
- Submission processes
- Cost of publication
- Open access or paid access
- Journal impact factor or reputation in the field.

The Thesis Whisperer contains an article about writing a journal article, from start to finish, in one week. [11] As part of that resource, it is recommended to consider all of the points above **before** you start writing. I think that is great advice. But I have also seen researchers make those decisions before they start and then change.

Once you start writing, the evidence can sometimes take you in a different direction. The main reason for this is the article reads differently on paper than what you expect conceptually. This means you can end up in a vortex or move in concentric circles: a process where you write then change your ideas on where the work might be submitted for review and publication. This leads to changing what you have written to account for style, word count or focus, which can have a knock-on effect forcing another decision change. Then you're back at the start modifying your idea. Hopefully, when you are caught in such a vortex you spiral outwards rather than inwards.

Writing is rarely a solo task.[12] Invariably you will have undertaken collaborative research and so your collaborators become co-authors. They may have different views on journal selection, writing style and the focus of the research. Although you can discuss these things during the collaboration, they are not always in your control.

## JOURNAL SELECTION

At this point, if you have not already selected the journal for review, you now face an important decision with big implications. Journal choice impacts earlier decisions such as:

- Word count
- Style and layout of figures
- Referencing style
- File sizes
- Typography
- Spelling and grammar (Australian, UK, US).

As noted earlier, there are other considerations before you select a journal. These include:

- **Impact factor:** Does the journal have an impact factor with which I am happy? Does it fit with my overall career development desires? Does it matter?
- **Standing in the field:** Where does the journal stand in my field? What about the fields of my collaborators?
- **Review process (including duration):** Is the review process well described? Do I trust the review process? How long is it, and can I afford to wait that long?
- **Paywall:** Are the published articles behind a paywall? Does that fit with the requirements of my funding body? Does that fit with my preferences/ethics?
- **Cost:** How much does publication cost? Are the fees fixed or variable depending on article length, use of colour or inclusion of figures?
- **Print, electronic or both:** Does the journal have a print and electronic version? Do I want to publish in print/online?
- **IP:** Who owns the IP of the article? Can I use figures elsewhere or not?

Of course, your views, and the views of your collaborators could be divergent, so you need to be prepared to make an argument, do more work, compromise or combination of all three.

## REVIEW

Once you select the journal and submit the manuscript for review, the rest of the process is out of your control. You cannot select the reviewers; you cannot change the review timeframe; and you cannot influence acceptance or rejection.

The review process leads to one of four possible outcomes:

- Outright rejection
- Request for revision and then resubmission for review
- Acceptance with minor revision and no further review
- Immediate acceptance (the unicorn of the research world).

The first three require further work. At the very least, it will be a rebuttal or rework of the manuscript. At the most, it will be conducting more experiments or new work and a complete re-write of the manuscript. Again, you need to take into account the views of the collaborating authors. Once complete, you climb on the review train again and subject yourself to further scrutiny.

# CHAPTER 4

# THE OLD PARADIGM
# IS SHIFTING

The old ways of doing things are (clearly) out. Only a small percentage—perhaps those at the top of their game at the latter stages of their career—can afford to act as they always have. For the rest of us, we live in a VUCA world:

- **Volatile:** At best, the values of grant schemes remain unchanged. However, they are often reduced in actual or real dollar value. Requirements for promotion are changing with increased emphasis on working with industry, yet few assessments, promotion or recruitment panels are considering this.

- **Uncertain:** With each change in government, research policy and/or funding seem to also change. This is true of both state and federal governments. Good programs are put on hold because they were *not invented here,* and there are no programs to follow in their place. This leaves further funding voids.

- **Complex:** Funding, research success, and academic progress are dependent on many moving parts. Was the grant well written? Do I have the most appropriate equipment and reagents? Are my students and staff prepared? What is my teaching load like this year? Is a restructure planned? Will there be changes to research support services? It is difficult to keep track of all of these variables, let along manage, control or respond to them adequately.

- **Ambiguous:** Often, the work we do or the contexts we work in can have many different meanings. What appears as a well-justified budget to one person looks completely unrealistic to another—and that is before you submit the application. The same is also true for the peer review process: the more we are asked to collaborate with people in our field, the more people are conflicted when it comes to reviewing our work.

These traits are well captured in the following diagram from an article in the Harvard Business Review in 2014.[13]

| COMPLEXITY | VOLATILITY |
|---|---|
| **Characteristics**: The situation has many interconnected parts and variables. Some information is available or can be predicted but the volume or nature of it can be overwhelming to process. | **Characteristics**: The challenge is unexpected or unstable and may be of unknown duration, but it's not necessarily hard to understand; knowledge about it is often available. |
| **Example**: You are doing business in many countries, all with unique regulatory environments, tariffs, and cultural values. | **Example**: Prices fluctuate after a natural disaster takes a supplier off-line. |
| **Approach**: Restructure. Bring on or develop specialists and build up resources adequate to address the complexity. | **Approach**: Build in slack and devote resources to preparedness—for instance, stockpile inventory or overbuy talent. Those steps are typically expensive; your investment should match the risk. |
| AMBIGUITY | UNCERTAINTY |
| **Characteristics**: Casual relationships are completely unclear. No precedents exist; you face 'unknown unknowns'. | **Characteristics**: Despite a lack of other information, the event's basic cause and effect are unknown. Change is possible but not a given. |
| **Example**: You decide to move into immature or emerging markets or to launch products outside your core competencies. | **Example**: A competitor's pending product launch muddies the future of the business and the market. |
| **Approach**: Experiment. Understanding cause and effect requires generating hypotheses and testing them. Design your experiments so that lessons learned can be broadly applied. | **Approach**: Invest in information—collect, interpret, and share it. This works best in conjunction with structural changes such as adding information analysis networks that can reduce ongoing certainly. |

**FIGURE 6:** VUCA CATEGORIES AND HOW TO RESPOND

# PUBLISH OR PERISH IS NOW
# PUBLISH AND PARTNER OR PERISH

Publish or perish describes the life of a researcher in an easy to remember catch phrase. This is not a new concept or idea to researchers; its early use can be traced back to 1942 ... yes ... 1942,[14] and I wrote about it in Chapter 3.

The implication being that if researchers do not have their work accepted in peer-reviewed journals, they cannot expect to have a very long research career. This is as true now as it was in the 1940s. Some would argue it is even stronger today.

Today, however, I think a few more 'P's are added to the mix:

- Be **Prolific**: It is no longer sufficient to publish. You need to publish often. Researchers need to publish more than ever before. Since the 1980s, researchers have been co-authors on more papers when compared to the period prior to the 1980s.[15] In certain disciplines, the expectation is for researchers to be part of at least three peer-reviewed articles per year. [16] In 2012, the University of Aberdeen suggested this number be 3.25.[17]

  However, when thinking about how prolific you should be as a researcher or how prolific your employer is asking you to be, it is worth considering the total research publication output. In 2007, across all research, there was an average of about 0.18 papers per researcher (1.3 million papers, 7 million researchers). In 2006, the average number of authors per paper was just under five. Taking that into account, the average number of papers on which a researcher would be an author, in any one year, would be 1. In 2014, an article published in Science suggested there are about 15 million researchers in the world, and 1 percent of those (about 150,000) have their names on 41 percent of all papers and on 87 percent of the most highly cited works.[18]

The report also looked at authors on multiple publications in one year:

- Two or more: 68,221
- Three or more: 37,953
- Four or more: 23,342
- Five or more: 15,464
- Ten or more: 3,269.

This data is interesting as it shows the VAST majority of researchers are not frequently publishing the work they undertake—certainly not in peer-reviewed journals anyway. Yet expectations of volume still abound. What is evident, however, is publishing 3–5 papers per year puts you well ahead of most other researchers (co-authored or single-authored). Three to five papers per year is 15–25 times the average publication rate.

Of course, today with social media, prolific publishing should include open access journals as well as blogs and other commentary that is directly accessible, without subscription, to the general public or informed end users (e.g. government policy makers in the case of health management research).

- Engage new **Partners**: Lone-wolf research is no longer acceptable. There must be collaboration. Furthermore, collaborations need to be with end users, not other researchers. Although Nobel prize winners are more likely to be lone-wolf researchers, the publication data supports an increase in collaboration. Fanelli and Lariviere (2016) point out that as publication rates have increased, so have co-authors. They even go as far as to say that if productivity is measured fractionally (½ a paper if you are one of two authors) then publication rates are steady, and collaboration rates are up.[19]

There is a large push in Australia and internationally to have more impact. Essentially, this means working more closely with end users, outside of research, so that your research is valuable to more than the research community. Researchers are increasingly asked to develop industry engagement skills in order to have greater impact or a defined pathway to impact.

Of course, working with industry partners—or even just new or different research partners—often implies the requirement for a different approach, different focus or both. Although the approaches or foci may not be materially different to the research conducted in the absence of the partnership, working collaboratively is definitely different to working alone.

Furthermore, taking on a collaboration often means removing something from your existing work. Have you ever met a researcher who says, 'yes, I've got spare time to take on more work or more collaborations'? All researchers operate at 100 percent and to take on new work would require them to operate at 110 percent or stop some work. It would be like packing more clothes into an already full suitcase where you eventually work out you either need a larger suitcase (more time) or you need to take out some clothes (do less).

On the flip side, there are researchers who treat industry partners like footy cards—something to be collected and hoarded. Partnerships are closely guarded. However, collecting, hoarding and guarding partnerships only serves to block the pathway to impact.

- Talk to the **Public**: The majority of fundamental research is conducted using government funds. As governments are asked to justify their spending including research spending decisions, researchers are expected to help in that process. This means working through open communication channels such as Facebook, Twitter and LinkedIn to reach the public. It means being active on these platforms and pursuing new ones such as Instagram, Snapchat and Reddit, as the public shifts in its use of social media. It means using blogs, newsletters, mainstream media and social media stars to communicate the importance of research—from *why* through to *why not.*

Although not every researcher has to be savvy on any one platform, most researchers will need to be active on at least one or they run the risk of being left behind in terms of funding or prioritisation.

The requirement to talk to the public does not end there. The model of research being published in pay-per-access journals is becoming increasingly unacceptable to government-funded research. The public, and, therefore, government, is demanding access to the research findings it funds. These open-access funding models require upfront payment from researchers. In some cases, such an approach prevents publication, in other cases, it diverts research funds to publication rather than more research. It's a bit like journalists paying to have their reports/articles published in newspapers so that readers do not have to pay.

Finally, electronic newsletters and blogs (as well as platforms such as Research Gate[20]) are allowing researchers to put their findings into the public domain quickly and easily, albeit with a requirement for some training or outside expertise. However, it is also allowing the public to have its say, forcing competition for audience share as well as message cut-through. Take, for example, the vaccination debate and associated MMR (Measles-Mumps-Rubella) vaccination's relationship to Autism. Although researchers have not been able to find links between the two—including studies showing similar communities with and without the MMR vaccine having had no effect on Autism rates—non-researchers still have significant sway with large parts of the community on the topic. Hence, MMR immunisation rates are dropping below ideal thresholds and allowing a rise in the incidence of measles.

## ANYONE CAN SELF-PUBLISH

The biggest disruption to research publication is new media. It is not that we need to produce, write, promote or connect to the public more effectively. Internet and associated platforms allow anyone to publish their thoughts on any topic, and these thoughts can then be viewed and followed by anyone else on the internet, anywhere in the world.

Blogs (WordPress is a specific example, but Facebook and LinkedIn also allow publication of blog-style content) demonstrate how easy it is for anyone to publish their research—particularly case studies. Now, people all over the world are documenting their lives on the internet. People are self-publishing their pathway through cancer, depression, pregnancy, childbirth, parenthood, moving house, renovating, and buying clothes. Everything is able to be blogged about. There are even communities devoted to documenting the process of opening new stuff—called unboxing[21]—including capturing and describing smells. Those blogs are easily found and the authors are easily identified. As a result, the easiest to find, read and understand become experts. That is, they become the go-to people on the issues contained within their blog. This is especially true in the absence of others to debate their expertise.

This means, that as researchers, there are many experts (bloggers) with case studies (blogs) available for anyone to find and read. However, that's all they have ... case studies. One experience in a sea of experiences. They cannot be stopped. They cannot be changed. As researchers, we need to live with them, be aware of them and know how to respond when we are asked about them. More importantly, in order to help inject evidence and rigour into the sea of opinion, researchers need to become one of those voices, knowing they have many cases studies—not just one.

## NEW MEDIA IS DAUNTING

Of course, if the public can self-publish, so can researchers. Although you may think that's just another thing to update, it doesn't have to be. Indeed, perhaps having your own web page or blog could replace large chunks of content on your university webpage. Perhaps your university page could link to your webpage and vice-versa. Your whole academic life could be documented on your webpage and be available for anyone to access. It would mean that when you change jobs or change universities, there wouldn't be an issue: just point your website to your new university page and vice versa, and you're ready to go. It's cost effective (less than $100 per year) and you'll have a great site. It's also easy and you'll go from nothing to published in an hour, or less if you have already documented what you want to achieve.

Of course, there is more to new media than blogs. There is Facebook, Twitter, LinkedIn, YouTube, Snapchat, Reddit and many others. You can do all of your blogging free via one or more of those platforms. However, most people don't. Data from 2012 suggest that only 1 in 40 scholars are active on Twitter, [22] with the largest proportion being Early Career Researchers.[23] Strikingly, 80 percent of academics on Twitter found it useful for their academic work, compared with only 25 percent who found academia.edu useful.

Many don't use social media because they are concerned: What if something happens? Remember, you don't matter, they're not listening and no one cares. Of course, the better option is to plan your response for 'when something happens' and to bear in mind that if you wouldn't say it in a crowded room, don't say it on the internet.

Shifting to using new media is a bit like the shift to a paperless office. At first, you find yourself printing out papers at home railing against the idea of reading articles on a screen/device and you refuse to use new media/social media. Eventually you find there are electronic ways to highlight text. Tweeted and blogged articles get more citations than their non-blogged or un-tweeted counterparts and the cataloguing of significant research is much easier using electronic systems than paper ones: you get instantaneous answers to questions from eminent researchers who have never responded to your email, but always reply to your tweet.

To put it another way, we have all experienced the steep learning curve on any new skill. For many, you need to learn the language and the process/skill. Take, for example, sport. You need to learn the terminology and rules used (language) as well as the techniques (specific skills) required to participate effectively. For musical instruments, you need to learn to read music (language) as well as what is required to produce a note, a series of notes, and ultimately, a tune (skill). Although we may be familiar with the sport (we've watched it on TV) or instrument (we've seen it played before), we acknowledge there will be a delay between time spent learning and our perception of the usefulness of the new knowledge we are gaining.

**FIGURE 7:** HAPPINESS AND THE LEARNING CURVE

However, our familiarity with the technological side of social media makes us somewhat impatient when it comes to social media. We expect to get it straight away. When, as mentioned above, there is a delay between time invested and skill/ability and ultimately value derived. Indeed, this has been nicely summarised by andfaraway.net[20] in respect of Twitter (see figure 8).

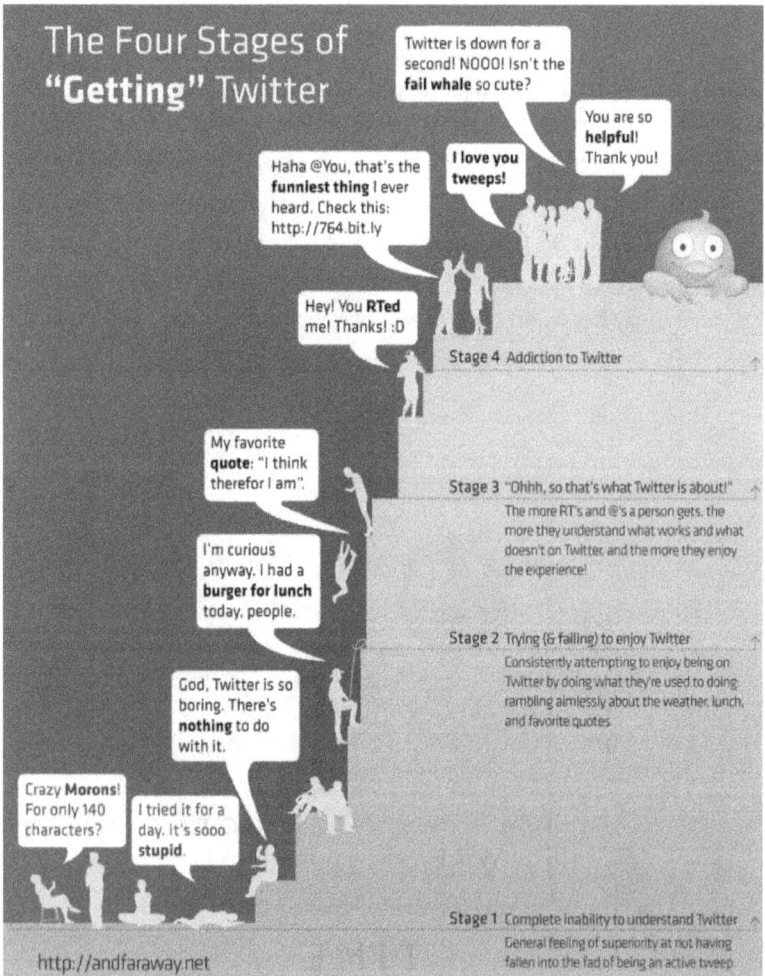

**FIGURE 8:** THE TRIALS OF TWITTER

## INFORMATION IS EASIER TO FIND AND ACCESS

For most of the history of research, information has been held in journals and books. Although individuals can purchase these, the reality is that most are/were limited to inclusion in major state, national or university libraries. As such, access was limited to those who were willing or able to have a membership as well as make the trip to the library, search the library database and then locate the item. Overall, it was a very time consuming and effort-filled process.

Although most research information is still housed in journals and books, and state or federal libraries and universities have paid for them, they are increasingly accessible. As researchers, if your information is not on the internet, or more specifically not indexed by Google, it can be difficult to find. The internet has put all data and information at our fingertips; Google ensures searching for this data and information was/ is easy and the indexing of research information in Google Scholar has made sure the public can also search research data.

This means that non-researchers can easily find and review information and become experts in a field without undertaking the extensive training that was previously required. MOOCs (Massive Open Online Courses) are a prime example of this. Students from around the world can access the best courses (Robotics at Stanford University) free. You might not get the paper certification at the end, but you have access to all of the relevant content and resources like any other student.

# MORE RESEARCHERS ARE BEING TRAINED

It is no secret that more and more researchers are being trained than ever before. According to UCUBE (official Australian University data as reported to the Department of Education), between 2010 and 2015, postgraduate research enrolments increased by between 1.3 and 6.5 percent (on the year before), to the point where there are now more than 65,000 new postgraduate research enrolments each year in Australia.[24] Completion rates, which are arguably a better measure, have grown between 1.3 and 5.3 percent and are now about 6,700 per year. This compares to annual university staff growth of between 0.6 and 3.7 percent over the same period and a total of 120,688 staff employed in the higher-education sector (head count growth of between several hundred and 4,000 per year).

Clearly staff growth of up to 4,000 per year does not match the 6,700 PhD completions per year.

On top of that, research funding, although not shrinking, is not growing to keep up. As a result, the notional total funding available per active researcher is going down.

All of this has led to a range of calls for major changes to the way research is funded. For instance, funding people not projects, shorter proposals, two-stage application process, and direct funding of research institutes/universities in order to reduce the number of PhD students enrolled per year.

If you are already in research or are one of the thousands of PhD students currently undertaking research training, you will be experiencing a competitive market with double the number of applicants to growth in research/university positions. The average growth over 5 years to 2015 was 2,000 per year, compared to average job seekers at approximately 4,000. [25]

So, I've just outlined a bunch of problems with research:

- The rapid growth in qualified researchers
- The slow growth in positions available
- The even slower growth in funding for research
- The need to publish online and in journals
- The need to collaborate, manage, grow, learn, maintain interest and change with the times.

So what next? How should you respond? How could you respond? How can you use your academic training to respond? How could you stay within your comfort zone (to a degree) yet still change?

# CHAPTER 5

# STOP PLODDING

Over the years, I've seen different researchers at various levels of comfort when it comes to positioning: from Plodder to Player to Performer and finally Positioned (see figure 9). Each level describes where researchers might find themselves and how that might impact their success (in research or translation) and how they might be perceived by others.

| Type | Funding Success Rate | Collaborative Opportunities | Perception | Impact | |
|------|------|------|------|------|------|
| Performer | 1:2 | 100% | Leader | Attract | Authority |
| Player | 1:10 | 40% | Likable | React | Anonymous |
| Plodder | 1:20 | 10% | Lagging | Repel | Anonymous |

**FIGURE 9:** PLODDING TO POSITIONED MATURITY MODEL

The model is a little like the transition a researcher might make as they move from PhD student to ECR, Postdoctoral and then Professor. Their work, knowledge and reputation increase within the academic circles they keep. However, in this case, they are concerned with translating that academic reputation into a wider reputation for knowledge and excellence within the end-user community and perhaps the public.

# PLODDER

The temptation is to think that Plodders are those just starting out in research, who perhaps had a helicopter supervisor. [26] They may have had few, if any, grant writing or collaboration forming opportunities, but they are not defined by lack of experience. They are the people, who despite experience and opportunity still do the same things that have not really proven to be effective for them or for others. It's a bit like the proverbial worker who blames their tools for poor performance.

On some level, Plodders know what they should do, so they just do it. Although they are on Twitter, they do not tweet. Their idea of talking with industry is to chat with one person, once, hear 'no' and decide industry is not interested.

They apply for grants but lament the lotto-like nature of the system and long for the days when good research was funded.

Although Plodders might have a successful research track record, they are wedded to the idea of communication with other researchers only. They do not see the value in trying to engage or work with others, and their idea of being on social media is to have a social media account.

Plodders have failed to see or respond to the shift in focus to accessible research regardless of the topic. They do not see that even within scientific writing (journal articles), the use of established story telling techniques, previously reserved for community engagement, positively impact citations.[27] Researchers 'can engage readers and increase uptake by incorporating narrative attributes into their writing styles'.[28] Factors such as sensory language, conjunctions, connectivity, and appeal all contribute to the narrative index and positively correlate with citation frequency.

In large-scale multi-organisation research projects, the support teams, also called professional staff, are often charged with making the science accessible by plotting a pathway to impact. In one such example, the ARC Centre of Excellence for Integrative Brain Function instituted an in a nutshell policy.[29] All articles produced by centre researchers would be summarised in a paragraph. The professional staff would undertake the work but it required interaction with the researcher, at least an interview, sometimes several. Although put forward as a program for increasing non-researcher engagement with the centre, many of the centre's researchers commented on the value of the in a nutshell policy when understanding the research of other academics in the centre. The lay-summaries were useful to a highly specialised audience.

Plodders rail against these ideas; they somehow believe that the complex should remain, and if you cannot understand it, then it's your problem not theirs.


# PLAYER

Players say the right things but do not always follow through. They are aware of the rules of the game and sometimes manipulate the rules to their advantage. For example, they might have received well-meaning but poor advice to say 'yes' to every offer or request for a partnership from an industry partner. At first, they are seen as a 'get things done' kind of person. Particularly when many other researchers say 'no', reluctantly say 'yes' or, worse still, ignore the request all together.

However, this can quickly turn to trouble. Saying yes to everything can result in being overloaded with work and struggling to meet the various deadlines and requirements of each project.

You may be meeting the deadlines, but are struggling to achieve the necessary quality measures. Perhaps you are not including all necessary controls, not quite achieving the number of survey respondents envisaged or including unnecessary questions in a survey, annoying respondents and, therefore, the industry partner. You might not even be the correct expert; saying yes might seem right (e.g. cancer expert for a potential cancer application), but the potential partner actually needs a formulations expert.

In a sales environment, this is the equivalent of a salesperson who promises everything, then is absent when the goods or services are delivered. You feel like you bought A but you are receiving B. We've all had this experience. We call up the telco and we explain our telephone and internet needs, then we receive our bill only to find out we did not quite get what we wanted. The salesperson promised everything, but delivered nothing.

Of course, there are other examples. A client came to me noting the difficulty he had faced engaging university researchers. On further interrogation, it was not so much a difficulty engaging them, but a bad experience leading to limited trust. He had engaged an expert to analyse a protein mixture. The aim was to identify the active ingredient in the mixture. A range of purification and analysis techniques were used and the supposed active was isolated. However, further analysis by a different laboratory revealed the wrong molecule was isolated. My client's university partner had actually isolated a reagent in the process not an active ingredient in the protein mixture. Upon further investigation it was found that the researcher was not an expert in the relevant field and they had used PhD students (even more inexperienced in the relevant research techniques) to undertake the purification and analysis.

In this example, the researcher would have been better to refer my client elsewhere than take on the project.

So, rather than always saying 'yes' to the work, say 'yes' and/or 'no' but only in order to better help the potential partner find the right expert. You will be known as helpful and will become a source of trusted advice.

# PERFORMER

Performers walk the talk; they recognise that gaining and maintaining industry or collaborative relationships takes continuous effort. They are in regular communication with their current collaborators and those whom they view as future collaborators.

They are the researchers who see the value in chatting with suppliers at academic conferences. They know that friendly relationships will put them in a better position when it comes to discussing commercial or collaborative opportunities—not just a cheaper price on their next purchase.

For many Performers, they have not consciously arrived at this position. Rather, they are people who intuitively work the room. It is something they have done their whole life from high school, through university and now as a career researcher. Their connections are not necessarily deep and meaningful, but they are valuable to all involved.

For other Performers, they have seen a formula that can help them achieve success. Unlike the Pretenders, these people know they need to say 'yes' and follow through. They also know that success comes from doing the numbers. They know that success is not just about having a good pitch; it is also about pitching enough times. It is about talking to enough people, getting to know what people want for themselves and their business or industry and then acting on it.

Performers, like elite athletes, artists and musicians, not only visualise their success but also the process. They see themselves making the calls, having the meetings, writing the proposals and ultimately doing the research.

In their book, *Will it make the boat go faster?* Ben Hunt-Davis and Harriet Beveridge explain how the success of the 2000 UK Olympic rowing team was based on process, not on outcome. They focused on the things they needed to do to be successful: their training, their strength and their rowing stroke rate. Although it was important to compete in lead-up events, they did not focus on what success would look like.

As a Performer, it is important that you do not focus on the number, size or duration of potential industry projects. Rather, focus on the number of people you meet, their problems, and how frequently you meet. It will multiply your chance of success in three ways:

- **Networking:** You will build your network of industry contacts. You will not be limited to a handful of people with whom you did your undergraduate degree.
- **Issues:** You will quickly identify common industry issues, meaning you will be better able to describe industry-relevant projects.
- **Accessible:** You will be viewed as an approachable researcher. A researcher worth spending time with or working with because you have listened in the past. You will be top-of-mind when there is a problem that only research can solve.

# PART TWO:
## GETTING POSITIONED

# CHAPTER 6

# ACADEMIC PERFORMANCE
# IS STILL THE BASIS OF SUCCESS

Within academia, researchers rarely sell themselves. Furthermore, if they do sell themselves, they do not see themselves as a salesperson or as selling. Neither is selling part of the academic research curriculum, and nor should it be.

Academic researchers are not selling anything. Their focus is on their area of interest and doing the best research possible. They are not selling their expertise or end research. In general, academics and researchers focus on positioning themselves relative to their peers and their field of interest. It is this process and associated activities that academics should focus on when it comes to attracting and maintaining partnerships with industry.

In academic terms, being positioned is the confluence of three activities:

- Applying for and winning competitive research grants
- Publishing your findings in peer reviewed journals
- Presenting your work at national and international conferences.

Being successful in these three areas provides a solid foundation for a fantastic academic career. That does not mean other areas such as education, research training, and outreach or community involvement are not important to academic success. It's just that, in my view, competitive grants, peer-reviewed articles and conference presentations are sufficient to position an academic as an expert in their field.

As the cadence of papers, publications and presentations increase, so does your positioning. There will be a continual but subtle shift from you asking people to work with you to responding to others wanting to work with you. This is the shift from recruiting to responding. A similar shift will also happen in relation to hiring staff. At first, you will advertise, then people will approach you directly to work with you or in your team(s).

It's a bit like high performing sports teams. Wins (and indeed premiership wins), increase how many players are willing to play for that team and perhaps at a lower price or higher entry fee. There are also organisations that are able to achieve the same outcome, not to mention high performing music or artistic teams.

However, being a high performing academic does not guarantee industry engagement. Nor does it guarantee you are seen as an expert by anyone other than academics in your field. For translational success, you need to be considered an expert in your field by people outside your field and people outside your sector.

So how can academics achieve this without selling? The following sections outline the factors I think are essential to success in translating your academic expert positioning into other sectors and fields. It is based on my experience, over the past 10 years, helping academics achieve research and translational success.

Without a doubt, high academic performance is still the basis of translational success. By translational success, I mean being able to work with industry partners for profit or for purpose, in the application of your knowledge and expertise to their problems. That is, you need to have academic quality and credibility in order to have success within the conversation or interaction.

However, we are not talking about being a professor or even an associate professor or having an outstanding academic career as rated by your peers. What we are talking about is being an expert in your field. The good news is that having a PhD should have already positioned you as the expert in your field—certainly on the topic of your PhD.

Why do I think this? Why am I so sure this is the case? Why is a PhD sufficient to be an expert? In my view, there are four reasons for this:

- **New knowledge:** PhDs are all about the generation of new knowledge. By definition, that means you should be one of a handful of people, in the world, with that specific knowledge.
- **Authority:** The data is clear. There are brands, people and roles we innately trust. This isn't because we know them, but because they have established themselves in our psyche as trustable. Included in that list are doctors, not just medical doctors, but anyone with a PhD. Thus, the title of a PhD positions you as an expert to others.
- **Training:** The PhD process teaches you a new way of thinking. It also teaches you ways of collecting, analysing and interpreting data that allow you, rapidly and accurately, to assimilate new information into existing thinking. In many cases, this can be outside your preferred area.
- **Experienced experts:** There are many experts in their field without PhDs: sports people, musicians, media stars, business people, and entrepreneurs. However, what is common to all of those groups is experience and expertise. Thus, regardless of your qualification, focusing for more than three years on the same topic is sufficient to be an expert. You have not just seen or read about the changes, you have lived through them and applied the solutions to fix them.

Good academic performance includes great research, but it also includes fantastic educational achievements, and a track record of supervising students to completion and supporting other researchers achieve their publication and competitive grant funding goals. All of these are necessary to further your academic career, and position yourself as an expert to those outside academia or research.

## RESEARCH PERFORMANCE

Research performance is evidenced in a range of ways: peer-reviewed publications, competitive grants and conference presentations.

### PEER-REVIEWED PUBLICATIONS

Central to effective academic positioning is the peer-reviewed publication. They help you demonstrate to your peers, inside and outside academia, how good your research is. They demonstrate both research quality and the impact of the findings to your field and/or sector.

However, they cannot be considered a short-cut to translation or engagement. Rather, they are an example of what you can achieve. If research translation were a paragraph of text, the research paper would be the exclamation point at the end of the last sentence of the paragraph. They are not the paragraph itself, or even the last sentence.

Instead of being put forward as the direct example of your work, peer-reviewed publications should be used as the evidence of your expertise. So, write a blog on the topic and reference the paper. Or write a story about the process of researching and writing the paper, and then reference the paper. You might even create a video covering the research findings, the research process or the research value/impact in context. It might be a bit like writing a literature review, where a point is made and backed-up by the suitable reference.

Regardless, you need to think about your peer-reviewed publications as the evidence of your work or your achievements, rather than the work itself. All you are trying to do is find a way to demonstrate your expertise, rather than always talking about your work.

## COMPETITIVE GRANTS

Competitive grants are the mainstay of a sustainable research program, group, team or career. Without success in competitive grants, there would be no research to translate, promote or position. Beyond the financial benefits of a competitive grant, they are also a key part of the academic promotion process, and form part of the metrics (both number of grants won and dollars raised) used to assess performance (just like peer-reviewed publications).

Importantly, industry partners intuitively understand the nature of tenders, requests for proposals and requests for quotations (see table 1). These all have many similarities to the competitive grant process that can be referenced or leveraged when looking to work with industry partners.

| FEATURE | GRANTS | TENDERS |
|---|---|---|
| Writing style is specific to the grant/tender body and project | Yes | Yes |
| Limited length | Yes | Sometimes |
| Restricted word count | Yes | Sometimes |
| Track record necessary for success | Yes | Yes |
| Rigid response templates | Yes | Yes |
| Strict submission deadlines | Yes | Yes |
| Application budgets are adjusted on approval | Yes | Yes |
| Short application timeframes | Sometimes | Yes |

**TABLE 1:** SIMILARITIES BETWEEN GRANTS AND TENDERS

Beyond the similarities with tenders, grants should also be viewed as evidence of your expertise. Like management consultants might refer to projects to demonstrate their track record, academics should refer to grants and the resulting research as an ability to design and deliver research projects, especially if the researcher is yet to have an industry project.

Of course, there are differences between grants and tenders of which researchers should be aware (see table 2). These differences are often laid bare when it comes to undertaking work with an industry partner. Industry partners expect the project to operate like a tender with regular updates, milestones and outcomes. Whereas, researchers expect it to operate like a grant; they will let you know when they are done and what they found.

| FEATURE | GRANTS | TENDERS |
|---|---|---|
| Reporting | Sometimes | Always |
| Specific outcomes must be achieved | Sometimes | Always |
| Progress payments based on deliverables | Rarely | Always |
| Milestone focused | Sometimes | Always |

**TABLE 2:** DIFFERENCES BETWEEN GRANTS AND TENDERS

## EDUCATION AND TRAINING

Other than research, another key element key of being an academic is to educate others. Even if you are a research-only staff member, the reality is much of your work involves education. You will be educating colleagues daily on the work you are doing. This will cover the methodologies you use, to the findings you make and the wider literature on your topic.

You educate students in your research team(s) or the students you directly or indirectly supervise. This includes presentations you give at conferences, journal articles you publish and the poster presentations you make. All of these things have educational components to them. Thus, when it comes to talking about yourself—for positioning purposes—your educational credentials are just as important as the research findings you make.

Of course, if you are a lecturer these activities are also opportunities to position yourself as an expert teacher in your field.

Regardless, in both scenarios it is possible to position yourself as someone who can educate others on a specific topic. That is, sharing your expertise with others as the translational outcome. Expertise in research methodology, expertise in training others, and expertise in a particular field all lend themselves to requiring a teaching component.

Just like research, education and/or training achievements are also a key part of academic progress. In particular, student supervision and lecturing are two areas of education and training that play a major role in academic promotion and, therefore, your overall positioning as an expert in your field.

Teaching students, particularly PhD students, can add further dimension to your academic program. Not encumbered by ways of thinking or the prevailing dogma, they can question the status quo in a way that can allow your research program or research thinking to develop.

However, seeing and/or using PhD students as cheap labour or the way to grow your research team is not advisable. A sustainable research group should consist of researchers at varying stages in their career, not just a cadre of students and a mid-level or senior academic.

# CHAPTER 7

# RELEVANCE: THE NEW WORLD ORDER

Now that we understand academic performance underpins excellent positioning, it is time to determine what is in and what is out. That is, being able to answer the question: what parts of my work are relevant to which industry partners? This is also the point where we are shifting from a sales strategy, to a content strategy. Sales strategies are where we tell people how good our product is and ask them to buy it. A content strategy is where we demonstrate our expertise in certain areas and ask them to work with us. This mindset shift is the key to positioning. Furthermore, this approach has a much better fit with the academic model of positioning for partnerships, rather than the commercial model of selling or marketing for partnerships.

As a successful researcher, you'll likely already have pretty good academic positioning. People in your field know you for your expertise and other personal traits (e.g. hard worker, good collaborator, diligent, thorough, critical thinker, well connected).

However, if you were to reflect on these relationships, you would probably soon realise that different people have a different understanding of your expertise. Some might see you as a methodological expert collaborating because of your ability to perform a particular technique or process. Others might see you as a technical expert with knowledge of the inner workings of a process, procedure, piece of equipment or machinery. Undoubtedly, there are people looking to ride on your coat tails, leveraging your success for their gain even though it might not be malicious.

Each of these academic collaborators has a different view on your expertise and, therefore, your relevance to them. In most, if not all, cases, these divergent views were not created deliberately. Rather, they were likely borne out of how you found them or they found you. For example, the first time they heard you speak might have been when you mentioned a new technique you mastered, a cohort you had engaged or a seminal finding you made. Of course, it might not have been a speech; it could have been a journal article, a student seminar or a poster presentation.

Similarly, you should not expect industry partners to have a consistent view of your expertise. Furthermore, how you position yourself will determine what elements of your research program and personality are viewed as attractive to potential partners. It's a bit like buying a car. You and your partner might agree on what you are buying, but not necessarily, why you are getting it. They might like the fact it's a hybrid. You might like the fact it has a sunroof. They might like the brand. You might like the styling. Ultimately, you are buying the same car, but you will talk about it in different ways.

Understanding your relevance is a three-step process:

1. **What I have:** your skills, expertise, capabilities etc.
2. **Who cares:** the people and organisations that might be interested in the above.
3. **Why they care:** What are their drivers for success, and how will you help them achieve their goals?

In the following sections, we will look at each of the three steps in more detail, and explore ways in which you can utilise them to attract industry partners.

## WHAT I HAVE

The first step in understanding your relevance is to identify your areas of expertise. The obvious place to look for your expertise is within your field of research. As noted above, this includes the projects you are conducting, your publications and grants.

Your projects, publications and grants will probably have different foci. Although they will have overlapping components, and show some kind of progression from one to the next. For example, grant -> project -> publication -> grant. Academic research is flexible; thus, you might choose to write a grant in a particular way because of the granting body's priorities. You might conduct the project in a particular way because your ideas on a future publication or grant will need certain information. The resulting publication might be written in a particular way due to the journal you are focused on, the grant you won, or would like to win, or factors such as collaborative authors and the number of times you have already submitted the article for review.

Your projects, publications and grants will also likely have different components or make use of different methodologies. Some parts will be collaborative or conducted by others who might be inside or outside your research team or group. Other parts will be your responsibility. Again, the justification for the differences might be pragmatic (e.g. reviewer preferences) or deliberate (e.g. your preferences or those of your collaborators) or environmental (e.g. that was what you had access to at the time).

When it comes to undertaking the research, there are likely parts that you could do but for various reasons others are doing them. Others may undertake certain parts, where you lack the necessary expertise. Similarly, when it comes to writing the journal articles, different people will take the lead on different aspects based on the work with which they feel most comfortable. For example, they undertook the experiment or are best placed to write as it fits more closely within their field of expertise than yours. Perhaps the journal is closer to their field of interest than to yours.

Thus, when documenting your expertise, you need to list what you are doing and what you are capable of doing. You should also consider the entirety of your expertise, not just the outcome of your work. For example, as a biochemist interested in cancer, you'll likely have preferred cell-systems and/or animal models you work with/on. Thus, your expertise should include the type of cancer you are interested in and the cellular systems and animal models you use in your work. Not to mention the various techniques you might employ such as protein/DNA expression/extraction: cell labelling or imaging.

As a social worker, you might be interested in the lived experience of people with a disability and, therefore, have expertise in qualitative and quantitative methods of data collection and associated analysis. Thus, your expertise extends beyond the lived experience of people with a disability. It also includes having good relationships with people with a disability, understanding qualitative data collection methods such as interviews and semi structured interviews, how to classify the data, and good interview and survey design.

For some, the best process to follow in documenting expertise is to review relevant source documents (e.g. grant applications, project descriptions and journal articles) and create a list in a spreadsheet. For others, a more visual approach such as a mind-map or sketch noting might be more appealing (see figure 10). Regardless of your preference, the important thing to do is make a comprehensive list—one that gives you the most options possible. At this point, nothing is out. If it helps your thinking and documentation process, note how each area of expertise is linked to the other. Does one thing flow from the next (e.g. data analysis follows data collection)?

It is important to be as specific as you can. Data collection is not sufficient. At the very least, you should talk about semi-structured interviews or online surveys. But computer assisted telephone interviews is even better. You might choose to categorise your expertise into different areas. Data collection might be one and data analysis might be another. Other high-level categorisations include stakeholder engagement, research communication, and education.

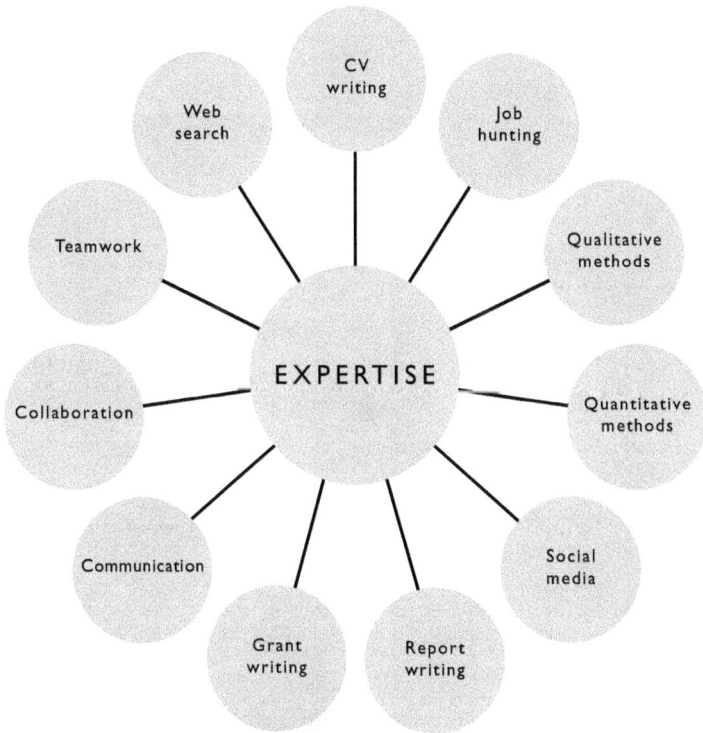

**FIGURE 10:** EXAMPLE MIND MAP OF MY EXPERTISE

# WHO CARES?

As a researcher, one of the toughest tasks you face is finding out who cares about your work. Unlike looking for grants, there are few lists of interested parties looking for research partners.

Finding out who cares about your research, should be approached like an investigative project. There are many ways to do this and many places to start. For example, you might:

- Talk to other researchers within your organisation and certainly within your sector. There are likely researchers already collaborating with your industry. Who do they work with? Why? Are there other industry partners in the sector who might be interested in your support? How did those researchers find their partners? Would that approach work for you? Bear in mind, you don't want to have these conversations and come across as wanting to take their partnership away.

- Review your previous partnerships. Have you had a previous grant, even as a partner investigator, that involved an industry partner? Why did they work on the project? Would they collaborate again? Don't assume the answer, directly ask the partner the question.

- Review your failed partnership attempts. When have you approached others? Why did they say no? How many have you approached? Could you change your approach to find out more about their needs and identify something they might care about?

- Perform an internet search based on your expertise identified above; search for key words. Discover who does the things you do. Identify the industries making use of your knowledge; list the companies and their locations. Do any seem like organisations you would like to or could work with? Contact them and chat about their work. Focus on finding out their problems, not pitching your research solution.

- Attend industry conferences not researcher conferences. Talk to attendees about their work and their problems, not your research solution. Grow your network. Follow-up with them at a later date.
- Review conference attendance lists. Can't make it to the conference? Have a look at who attended. Find their organisation and determine how they might work with you and vice versa. Reach out for a meeting to discuss their problems.
- Read sector review papers. Is the government talking about building your sector? Is there a sector development plan? Who was involved in the planning and writing? Would they meet with you? What about listed organisations?
- Read government policy papers. Do they refer to organisations? Do the papers imply policy changes or updates to process or procedure in your area of expertise? Which organisations want, need or could use that support?
- Respond to people interested in your social media profile or posts (e.g. LinkedIn or Twitter). Keep active on social media and respond to industry partners. When they connect, request a meeting to discuss their problems.
- Engage the relevant industry growth centre. In Australia, there are seven industry growth centres. Make sure you know to which growth centre(s) your work is aligned. Reach out to that centre(s) for a meeting with key staff and key participants. Attend their conference.

As with your expertise, making a list or map is important; so is categorisation. Such an approach will help with prioritisation. You might list all partners interested in your methodological expertise in one section and partners potentially interested in your subject matter expertise in another section.

# WHY THEY CARE

Academics in research spend many hours considering how others—particularly granting bodies—might be interested in their work. When it comes to national grants such as the National Health and Medical Research Council and the Australian Research Council and international grants such as Wellcome Trust, National Institutes of Health and the European Commission, researchers are well aware of what the priorities are.

In my experience, this is achieved in two ways. The first is the direct communication of priorities from the granting body to researchers via public announcements such as information sessions and posting the same or similar information to websites. For example, in the case of the NHRMC and the ARC, the Australian Government has set various national health priority areas.

The second way researchers understand priorities is through their own investigation. This is achieved by talking to representatives of the various granting bodies, and talking to successful and unsuccessful applicants about their proposals.

Together, these approaches give researchers a clear picture about the kinds of things their application should focus on. Invariably, this will influence the approach but not necessarily the focus of the research. That is, researchers will adjust their argument regarding the importance of their work, rather than change the focus of their work.

However, outside granting bodies, my experience suggests few researchers go to the same level of effort to determine industry partner requirements. Indeed, the approach taken is almost the opposite of that described above. Rather than wide consultation, researchers invariably rely on hearsay from one or two others and rarely make direct approaches to industry to determine their preferences.

Rather than asking for their requirements or responding to their needs, researchers tell industry about their fantastic work. How good the research will be for the industry or partner organisation. How, if they do not undertake this work or research, they will be at a competitive disadvantage.

## TREAT IT LIKE A GRANT

The problem is talking with industry should be no different to writing a grant. Just like writing a grant, talking with industry is a process that involves intent listening. Successfully working with industry relies on a deep understanding of their problems—just like understanding granting body requirements or research priorities. It is only once you understand industry priorities and problems that you can pitch a solution. Indeed, it is only at that point that you will fully appreciate how your expertise could be framed and thus how you can pitch your solution.

If the process of investigating granting body requirements involves reading grant guidelines, attending information sessions, seeking feedback on your applications and talking to other successful applicants, then question is what are the equivalents within industry?

| GRANT INFORMATION | INDUSTRY EQUIVALENT |
|---|---|
| Grant guidelines | Sector wide issues papers, direct chat with industry |
| Information sessions | Launch events for issues papers, industry conferences |
| Talking to successful applicants | Talking to people with industry partnerships |
| Application feedback from peers | Application feedback from potential funders |

**TABLE 3:** GRANT INFORMATION AND INDUSTRY
PARTNERSHIP EQUIVALENTS

Grant guidelines, particularly national or statewide priority areas are the equivalents of the issues impacting the sectors or businesses in which you are interested. Often, these priority areas are discussed in white discussion and issues papers produced by the representative bodies that cover your industry or sector. The priority areas might also be highlighted in reviews conducted by government on behalf of the sector. Talking directly to potential partners is also like obtaining the grant guidelines. Not all issues will be articulated in issues papers. Furthermore, many companies will not openly share their problems with the rest of their world, particularly if it could mean their competitive advantage is negatively impacted.

Granting body information sessions that are held to provide further or clarifying information in relation to national priority areas and associated grant guidelines are also present for industry partnerships. In this case, they look like information sessions or launch events for the various reports mentioned above. There are also industry conferences (not academic or research conferences). At these conferences, you can learn about the problems faced by industries and sectors and seek clarification, particularly in the context of further research, or how the issues have been or are being resolved. At these conferences, companies are also presenting their best products. By attending, you will get to see how various technologies are applied in the real world. Not to mention how what you might think of as cutting edge may be used (or not) across a particular sector.

Researchers will often talk to other successful research grant applicants and research offices often provide similar introduction services. The same approach can be used for industry partnerships where researchers share their successful (and not so successful) attempts at engaging and working with industry partners.

Finally, when researchers write competitive grants, other researchers listed on the grant invariably review the proposals. Furthermore, research offices also provide a blinded or semi-blinded peer review process. Again, a similar approach can be applied to industry engagement. However, it is necessary to bear in mind that grants are peer reviewed, thus a mock peer review process is entirely relevant. Therefore, a draft or developing industry proposal should be industry reviewed rather than researcher reviewed. That is, proposals (no longer than a page) should be shown to potential industry partners as part of the development process. This sharing should not be viewed as giving away intellectual property or the destruction of a relationship if it does not meet requirements. However, like all good draft proposals it needs to be well considered. You would not give a half-baked grant idea to senior researchers in your field to review and the same is true for industry proposals.

Just like a grant peer review process, showing actual or potential industry partners your proposals in development is about improving the proposal/idea. Thus, it is important the feedback provided is acted upon. As a researcher, you may be tempted to dismiss some of the comments as irrelevant to your work or the project. Perhaps you might even see the suggestions as materially changing the project. However, it is important to realise the purpose of these reviews is to improve the proposal from an industry perspective. Unlike a grant, if the review process takes the proposal away from your area of expertise, you should respond by notifying the partner of that fact. If necessary, it might even require a change to the personnel involved or referral to a new researcher all together. Although such a move might be disappointing at first, it positions you as trustworthy. Furthermore, it ensures you are able to deliver the industry project because anything you take on should fit within your area of expertise and associated capabilities.

## BUILD AN AVATAR

Another way to approach the problem of who cares is to create an avatar of your actual or potential audience. How old are they? Are they male or female? How long have they been in their role? Are they experienced? What sort of education and training do they have? Of course, do not forget to consider the organisation, industry or sector in which the avatar works. The more specific you can make your avatar, the better. As an example, in some sectors, avatars include music and food tastes. This information is then used to help win over the person or people involved in decision making.

## KNOW WHAT YOU'RE SELLING
## (AND WHAT THEY ARE BUYING)

As academics working with industry, we need to understand that what we are selling may not be what they are buying. It is a bit like the life hack videos popular on the internet. There are countless examples of adding magnets to clothes pegs and using them on white boards. So, people going out to buy clothes pegs may not be buying them to hang clothes. Instead, they could be buying them to create document clips for whiteboards. Knowing the buyer is using them for a whiteboard craft project would mean suggesting pegs with different properties than for hanging clothes. For example, you might suggest larger pegs, or ones with a flat surface that a magnet could be glued to. Whereas, if you were selling to someone using the peg for hanging clothes idea you might need to know if they will be used indoors or outdoors and how they might survive if accidentally left out in the rain or always left on the clothes line no matter what the weather.

Similarly, academics could be selling their expertise, yet industry might be buying their experience or vice-versa. Although it might not matter to you or your potential industry partner if they are not buying what you are selling, it is helpful to realise this difference. Indeed, academics who are clearly able to understand these differences will be best placed to work with industry. They will be talking a similar language, outputs and inputs. Just like knowing a peg will be used in a craft project will make it easier to sell certain types of pegs, knowing what your potential industry partner is buying will make it easier to engage with them.

## DO A LITERATURE REVIEW

All researchers have the capacity to deliver across the academic spectrum. That is, they can deliver education, research and training to organisations all based on their research expertise. It is just a matter of identifying what and how. To establish what they want, you'll need to perform a review. The first part will be a web-based search, using your expertise as the search term. It could be a question: how do I …?, a statement: the best way to …, or something else: troubleshooting …. The focus will be to identify companies or people using your expertise. Next, use this information to review the companies or people. What are they doing? What do they need? Where are they based? How do they fund their work?

## TALK TO INDUSTRY

Finally, make contact. Talk to users and potential users. Talk about your expertise. Listen to what they say. Do they want your expertise? Or do they want something else? As required, respond and change your description as you meet additional potential partners.

All the while, you will be keeping a record of what you have identified as the problem within the market place and the solution you could provide. It is worth considering how you might provide that solution. Three different areas of expertise are covered below.

## EDUCATION PROJECTS

Many researchers discount the value of their knowledge to potential industry partners. Having worked in an area for an extended period, constantly building their knowledge through review and application, and working with others at the same level many researchers feel their knowledge is not unique or valuable to others. In some sectors, researchers believe that industry is not after education, but rather solutions to problems: that industry would like new widgets. That industry would like a report.

However, researchers are a wealth of knowledge. They know how various machines operate. They know how to design good data collection projects. They know how to perform specific research techniques. All of these things are potential opportunities for researchers to work with industry, without focusing on performing research.

For example, a client in the 3D protein crystallography research space partnered with a pharmaceutical development company to crystallise and visualise their protein of interest. Although all parties agreed the project would take three years, the researchers felt the work could be conducted in as little as three months—and it was. Although the pharmaceutical company was pleased with the outcome, it was actually more interested in (and would have paid more) learning about why a process that was planned to take 36 months was completed in three. Luckily, the project had a spare 33 months as a result, providing space for the researchers to pass their protein crystallography knowledge onto the pharmaceutical company.

The education or training could also be the subject of your expertise. In the example above, the protein crystallography methodology was a means to an end; a tool the researchers used to achieve their goals. However, following their success, it is clearly a technique they could teach others to use for their own work and purposes.

In a separate example, I have worked with socially focused researchers who are academic experts in their field. Furthermore, much of the work they undertake includes interacting with and reviewing the performance of companies working in their industry. As a result, sharing the outcomes of their research has been relatively straightforward. They provide a report back to the participant organisations. However, the next obvious step was to provide training to bridge the gaps identified by the research. This lent itself to further research and training cycles where data could be collected to evaluate the impact of the training, refine the program and start again: a quality improvement loop where academics review performance and design interventions. Thus, although the participant organisations are very interested in the research, the ability to provide training and education was deemed far more useful than participating in the research itself.

## BODY OF KNOWLEDGE

For most researchers, the body of knowledge they access on a regular basis is extensive. The requirement to understand and orient their thinking and research findings to existing information is essential for success. For example, each talk, each peer-reviewed article, and each poster presentation requires an introduction: an orientation for the audience about the new work you will soon present to them. Not only that, talks, articles and other presentations also require a reframing of the knowledge base resulting from your findings.

This ability to understand and reframe context—context specific to a system, organisation, industry or sector—is a key skill that could be used as a primary industry engagement activity. The fundamental knowledge gained early in your career, perhaps as a graduate or post-graduate student, will be applied and referred to repeatedly. This knowledge and its application places you in a fantastic position to teach others the fundamentals that form the basis of their work, but not the work itself. It could be the theory of your process or system of interest or the research techniques you use. All have potential as education or training outcomes that engage industry.

For example, in the disability sector there is large focus on active support. That is, the provision of sufficient help for the person with a disability to be able to do as much as possible for themselves. The goal is to create a fulfilling independent life for them. However, it is a forgotten practice despite being well covered in relevant courses (e.g. social work degrees). When people enter the workforce, they find it easier to do the work than support the person with a disability. Rather than help a person feed themselves, the support worker will feed them. After time, the support worker completely forgets how to apply active support. A researcher or academic versed in the theory of active support would be well placed to provide workshops or training on implementing it. Indeed, this is the case for one of my clients, where they have achieved significant industry engagement through offering longitudinal active support quality improvement programs.

In another example, research training is the go to expertise for engagement. On Instagram @coffeesciencelab obtained her PhD in renewable energy. Yet, she is engaging coffee roasters, baristas and coffee enthusiasts because she recognised how this group of people value the research method: the systematic trialling and assessing coffee bean selection, roasting, grinding, extracting, pouring and tasting. @coffeesciencelab saw a dedicated group using trial and error to change the taste of coffee. She viewed this trial and error as research; however, it lacked an underlying system or process. Thus, quality and reproducibility of results was difficult. Knowledge of the scientific method was key to integrating in the community. Now @coffeesciencelab is considered a coffee expert. Yet, her background and training is in renewable energy and the expertise she brought to coffee-making was the scientific method.

## RESEARCH

Of course, there is also your research expertise. This is topic of interest for you; the cutting edge of which you sit at the forefront. It's what you publish journal articles on, present at conferences and what you spent four years researching as part of your PhD.

This is the most obvious space that researchers play in when it comes to industry engagement. For most, it is easy because it is something they are very comfortable talking or writing about. However, the easy part is most often in talking or describing. Focusing only on your research expertise as a point to engage industry partners is hard to achieve.

This is for several reasons:

- **You are the expert:** You are one of a handful of people who know your field in that detail. You might be the only person who knows the thing. However, this creates problems. If no one knows what you know, how do they know they need it? If there are few people who know the field in detail, how do you explain the problem or solution to them in terms they understand?

- **The pool of interested people is small:** I'm all for niche approaches to engagement. Indeed, narrowing down what you are able to offer makes it easy to specify who you might approach with your offer. Specify down to the individual level, not just sectors, organisations or role titles. However, if you're interested in a specific gut microbe, in a specific mammal living in a specific geographic location, there are likely few industry partners who will be interested in that. Conversely, what you know about the gut microbe, or the relevant mammal, or the region it lives in could all be factors of interest to an industry partner in their own right.

- **It is too familiar to you:** The regularity with which you speak and write about your research makes it familiar to the point where it is difficult to talk about the work in terms non-experts (inside or outside research) can understand. It takes a particular skill to switch from one audience to the other; it often requires the help of an independent third person to identify the jargon or inside language being used.

## HOW THEY WANT IT

Beyond what industry partners want, there is also the matter of how they want it.

Going back to our car example, you might buy it with cash, a loan, a novated lease or a line of credit. All have different structures and benefits for the buyer and seller. For the seller to know the buyer is using cash might mean they want to leave the showroom with a car on the day. If the buyer is using credit, the car may need to undergo an inspection from a finance company. Furthermore, if the buyer is not using cash, but does not yet have credit the car dealership might encourage seeing the finance area of the dealership. Then you need to take into account how the car is delivered or picked up, and the inclusion of a service and/or clean as part of a larger deal.

Similarly, when working with researchers, industry partners might be interested in different payment terms or options. They may want the project spread over six months, or completed within three weeks. They might want the work conducted at their site, at your site or at a third-party location.

As a researcher, looking to partner with industry, it is essential to be aware of these different possibilities. Although some might be difficult to accommodate, others will be easy. Be open minded about doing things differently, particularly when it will not impact the research outcome. If you do not understand their motives for a particular option or requirement—ask. If you could be more flexible in a particular area, but less so in another—let them know.

# CHAPTER 8

# CUT THROUGH

There are two components to cut through. The first is your message: what and how you say something. The second is where you choose to say it. In this instance, we are separating academic places to say something like journals or conferences from more public places like blogs or public meetings. Of course, the two are not mutually exclusive.

## MESSAGE

The message is not just what you say; it is also how you choose to say it. The climate change debate is full of failed attempts at convincing people of the science. However, through this debate we have come to realise that people are sold via story and convinced via science. Increasingly in this field, scientists, researchers and academics in general, focus on creating stories and metaphors that describe their work. They don't leave the heavy lifting to the data.

We know that in music and cinema, predictability results in disinterest. Think about the best movies. They are the ones with unseen twists. For music, it is about the beat and subsequent break beat that generates interest. Whereas, if we can predict the next part of a song—the beat—we think of it as being too simple. If it is hard to predict—the break beat—we think of it being too complex. In the former, we lose interest because it is too easy, and in the later, we lose interest because we cannot keep up and the beat is too hard to follow.

Scientists must think the same about their work. If they are always communicating in the same way—statement->method->evidence-> statement->method->evidence—the delivery can become predicable and uninteresting. Science has the added challenge in that the subject matter can be complex and difficult for non-expert audiences to understand.

This delineation of expert versus non-expert is often not limited to scientists or researchers versus non-scientists or non-researchers. In many cases, expertise is so niche that even other scientists or researchers find the content difficult to grasp. Summaries of research such as in-a-nutshell offered via cibf.edu.au on their research have proven useful to their participating and collaborating scientists to quickly understand the research underway across the centre. However, researchers can feel there is a risk of error if we oversimplify in order to make something more accessible/understandable.

A way around both of these problems—over simplification and the need for unpredictability—is story. Indeed, the in-a-nutshell makes use of story and metaphor to convey meaning. Story could be how the work came to be relevant. It could be how the work was undertaken (not the method). It could be a metaphor for the finding or the process. Nonetheless, it is about breaking up the expectation of what comes next and how predicable it might be in order to make it interesting. Remember, a story is about entertainment first and information second. This may be the opposite of what you are used to—information first (data, evidence, results) and without any focus on entertainment (how you got there). Furthermore, it is not just about making the content interesting, but the delivery too.

## LOCATION

The best-presented message to the wrong audience will not earn industry partners. Presenting research at academic conferences via presentations and posters will undoubtedly engage researchers. To the extent they attend academic conferences, potential industry partners may also look to form collaborations. However, with thousands of businesses in operation across Australia and many more across the world, it is impossible to get an audience with them all via academic conferences alone.

Indeed, researchers should embrace the world of new media and the internet. This allows one:many communication. The many could be an order of magnitude greater than at the largest conference. Furthermore, the communication can be asynchronous. Meaning, the message is delivered at a convenient time (i.e. when you are ready), and it is received at a convenient time (i.e. when they are ready). These two timeframes may be seconds, minutes, hours, days or months apart.

Of course, each new media channel (e.g. social media, YouTube, websites) has its own nuances, and it is important for researchers to recognise their differences. These differences include, but are not limited to:

- Audiences that are likely using each channel or sub-channel
- Kinds of content shared
- Social norms on each channel
- Limitations of viewing or sharing content.

## SOCIAL MEDIA

Social media is a large and ever-growing group of technologies. According to Sensis, in 2017 nearly 80 percent of the Adult Australian population used social media. The same report also indicated that 64 percent of respondents were more likely to trust a brand due to positive interaction on social media.[30] Therefore, social media is well entrenched in the adult Australian population, and it allows positive brand interactions in the absence of face-to-face contact.

The defining feature of any social media site or platform is the ability to share ideas, knowledge and information, electronically in a public fashion. Importantly, social media allows recipients to comment, share and like content with which they interact. This means the sharing of information is two-way, unlike a website, where viewers do not have an opportunity to comment back to content.

YouTube, Research Gate, LinkedIn, Twitter, and Facebook are examples of social media. Undoubtedly, researchers are active on all of these channels, not just as researchers but as private citizens. For some, this creates problems. The biggest question is do I have multiple accounts representing personal and work, or just one? Only the individual can answer this question. However, speaking from experience, having multiple accounts makes management more complex. Furthermore, you are one person with one life. For most researchers, although their work is their job, it is also their major passion. Thus, to separate work from the rest of life would take away a major passion from their social media stream. Of course, if you are not active on social media, joining one or more services and focusing on your research is a good place to start. Indeed the easiest way to separate personal from work social media is to separate across channels. For example, use Twitter for work and Facebook for personal.

However, before opening an account, it is important to think through how you will operate and manage it. For example, who is your target audience? Are you writing for other researchers or for industry partners? Who will you follow? Who would you like to follow you? How will you know when your actions are successful? How much time will you devote to the task?

You should consider all these things as they will help make being active easier. For example, knowing who you are writing for will determine what platform you chose first. It will also help determine what content to create and what content to share and re-post. It will help guide when and how you comment on other posts.

Knowing who you would like to follow, and who you would like to follow you is a great way to determine content. It also helps with whose content you share or comment on. Regardless of what social media platform(s) you choose/use, there some basics when it comes to establishing, growing and maintaining a following:

- **Follow people you know:** This includes research colleagues and friends. They will most likely follow you in return; however, in this case, follow has two meanings. The first is the social media meaning where their content appears in your feed: what you see on your home screen. The second is to look at what, when and how they post content and to emulate or avoid it. Use their accounts and content to guide what you like, love or loath.
- **Follow strangers:** By this, I mean follow accounts of people you don't know, but would like to have follow you. Again, follow is used with double meaning, first in the social media sense and second in the sense of a guide or teacher.
- **Follow the leader:** Who is the leader in your field or area? Follow them in both senses. If you want them to follow you, consider starting a social media chat with them in public. Keep it positive, upbeat, and informative. Think of the things your followers would like to know. Ask questions on those topics.

- **Ask for re-posts:** When you post content, ask your followers to re-post it. At the very least, include a line within your post that encourages further distribution.

- **Let them know you are everywhere:** Post to all of your social channels that you are on other social media channels and let them know how to connect with you on those channels. You should also do this with any oral or written presentations. Of course, some social media will be more or less appropriate in different circumstances. It will be up to you to determine where and when. In most cases, the purpose you have assigned to the particular account (see below) will determine when and how you mention it.

- **Post regularly:** Aim to post content daily (at least weekly), with original content (i.e. your own material) posted in only one in five posts. Indeed, reposting and cross posting content from one channel to another is a great way to spread knowledge and information.

Below I cover four social media platforms. I have chosen these based on their popularity and their usefulness to researchers. There are many more social media platforms, and you'll need to choose the one(s) that are best for you.

## INSTAGRAM

Instagram is a picture-based social media platform. Although you can include text, all posts must have an image. Of course, it is possible that the images are themselves text, like a slide from a presentation. In Australia, in 2017, 46 percent of people on social media use Instagram. This is up from 31 percent in 2016 and 26 percent in 2015. It is second to Snapchat in terms of percentage growth over that period.

## TWITTER

Twitter is a text-based social media platform. Each tweet is limited to 280 characters (up from 140 prior to 2016). Text can include links to documents, video, images and direct posting of images and videos. In Australia, 32 percent of people using social media use Twitter. That is up from 19 percent in 2016 and 17 percent in 2015.

## FACEBOOK

Facebook is arguably the quintessential social media platform and is used by 94 percent of Australians on social media. This percentage has remained steady since 2015. Posts can be about virtually anything, of any length, and can include any content – images, videos, original, reposts.

## LINKEDIN

LinkedIn is the only work-dedicated social media site with virtually no competitors. It is one of the few popular social media sites able to penetrate The Great Firewall of China.[31] In Australia, usage (as a percentage of people on social media) has dropped in recent years from 28 percent in 2015 to 24 percent in 2016 and 18 percent in 2017. Recent changes implemented by new owners, Microsoft, may reverse that trend in 2018.

| | INSTAGRAM | TWITTER |
|---|---|---|
| **USE IT BECAUSE** | It's popular, very visual, can add text to images. | Lots of academics do. |
| **AVOID IT BECAUSE** | Sharing other people's content is hard. As a result, some accounts appear narcissistic. | Users can struggle to understand it, and it has a culture that is difficult to learn unless you join the platform and participate. |
| **GROW FRIENDS BY** | Following anyone. | Following anyone. |
| **SHARE** | It's difficult to share other people's content without third party apps, every share has to include a picture, you cannot share short videos (less than 3 seconds), images must be a particular size or they are cropped, cannot click on shared links, characters limited to 2,200. | It's easy to share other people's content, limited to 280 characters (previously 140). Can have text, images, links, and videos. |
| **FINDING CONTENT** | Use #hashtags and accounts you find interesting. Difficulty in sharing and lack of links in content means finding content needs to be more active. | #hashtags and location-based searches. Tends to have event-based #hashtags and associated running commentary. Shares from the people you follow help broaden what you see. Tweet-ups (tweeting on a topic for an hour or so) are common. |
| **SUCCESS FACTORS** | Good use of #hashtags, appealing visual content | Good use of #hashtags, participating in tweetups, share-worthy content. |

| | FACEBOOK | LINKEDIN |
|---|---|---|
| **USE IT BECAUSE** | It's popular, visual, all forms of media can be shared. | It's work dedicated, lots of industry, limited active researchers (so you'll have lots of space with few competitors). |
| **AVOID IT BECAUSE** | Mixing business and pleasure can make it difficult to adequately engage your friends in relation to your personal life and your work colleagues in relation to your career. | Usage is dropping. As a senior researcher, you might find more unsolicited requests for work and 'coffee' than you would like. |
| **GROW FRIENDS BY** | Connecting with people you know. | Asking people you have worked with or would like to work with. You can follow people without being a connection. |
| **SHARE** | Easy to share other people's content, no character limit, can have text, images, links, and videos. | It's easy to share other people's content, no character limit, can have text, images, links, and videos. |
| **FINDING CONTENT** | #hashtags and location-based searches. Shares from the people you follow help broaden what you see. Lots of suggested content you might like depending on what you have liked and interacted with previously. Groups are very popular. | #hashtags. Shares from the people you follow help broaden what you see. Lots of suggested content you might like depending on what you have liked and interacted with previously. Groups are very popular. |
| **SUCCESS FACTORS** | Compelling content that encourages discussion and debate. Followers/friends who are willing to discuss and debate your posts without being a troll. | Participating in groups and discussions. Having a summary that represents you (particularly the future you). Posting short articles that resonate with your intended audience. |

# WEB PRESENCE

## BLOGS

As academics, we tend to have a singled-minded focus on our own work. This should not be confused with not being aware of the rest of the literature—of course, we are. However, it can come across as a little narcissistic within non-academic circles. Your approach to talking about your own work should be diluted by a factor of one in five.

It is also important to reference the work of others in the same manner that you talk about your own. This does not mean citing other people four to five times as much as citing your own work. Rather, and in the context of a blog, it means writing about the work of others four to five times as much as your own. If you write a blog every week, then once a month it would be about your work. The other times it would be about the work of others.

For example, if you are interested in cancer, your blog might focus on recent significant findings in cancer research. You could take a relevant piece of research (peer-reviewed journal article) and summarise it in 800 words or fewer using language understood by non-researchers. Like any review, you might write about the significance of the research, the difficulties the researchers might have faced/overcome. As with any good review, you would reference your sources. As it is a blog, and not a literature review, it does not need to have a full reference list (but references should be cited if used). It is also okay for it to be your opinion, rather than evidence-based. However, it is not a peer review. It is not a critique. It is not your opportunity to take down the research.

Then, once per month, you might focus on your own paper and adopt a similar approach to how you blogged about the papers of your peers. You could choose any topic you like. However, as with social media in general, having a defined purpose and ideal audience in mind is key to growing your audience. It is up to you how you make those decisions and what comes first: topic, purpose or ideal audience. You might go round in circles as you become clear on what is most important to you. Indeed, this might even happen as you write, particularly as you discover who reads them and what they get from them. Here are some topics (other than journal articles in your area of interest) you could include:

- Daily life
- Methodology
- Research/science in the media
- Your topic in the wider community.

Regardless of your intended audience, topic or purpose, you should aim to:

- Write regularly and frequently—once a month at least, but ideally once per week.
- Keep it short—no more than 800 words, and certainly no more than 1,000.
- Cross promote—copy and paste to places like LinkedIn, Facebook and Instagram, where longer posts are allowed. Share using Twitter.
- Repost—when you're not writing content, repost content written by others. Again, remember your audience, purpose and topic. Also, repost your own content.

## NEWSLETTER

Newsletters, like blogs, need a defined purpose, ideal audience and clear topic. Similar to blogs, they should be produced frequently and regularly. However, once a quarter might be enough for most, with once a month being the ideal target. For some people, centres, institutes or organisations, a weekly newsletter is considered ideal. However, that may require more work than people are willing to put in.

If you are writing a blog, you might decide to distribute it via a newsletter. In which case, your audience, purpose and topic will closely align with that of your blog. Being a newsletter, you may wish to include pertinent announcements such as events, significant discoveries, a preview of the next blog/newsletter, staff/researcher or collaborator profiles.

Many web-based programs can support the maintenance and curation of email lists for newsletters. Although hard copy newsletters might be nice to have, they can be expensive to create and distribute. Not to mention the difficulty of tracking how and when people interacted with them.

Conversely, most electronic newsletters (e.g. delivered by programs such as mailchimp, canva and salesforce) can be tracked and traced as clicks, reads, forwards and shares are all monitored and reportable. This makes understanding what content is resonating with which audience easier. Therefore, you can refine your content, purpose or audience to meet your needs or change your mind to deliver what the audience wants.

Above all, however, the newsletter should be easy to read. In paper or electronic copy, the document needs to be accessible. How do people get your printed newsletter? Can you send it to a better address? Is the address you have sufficiently detailed? For an electronic newsletter, is it filtered into SPAM? Can people read it in their email program? Do they need to click links to read specific content? Or is it all there? These things all have a bearing on engagement with your newsletter and, therefore, with you and your research.

Note that before you set out to send your newsletter to your email or postal list, make sure you are aware of the relevant privacy laws in your state/territory/country. In most cases, joining a mailing list is opt-in rather than opt-out. Thus, people must have actually signed up to receive your newsletter. This creates an interesting challenge for many in terms of getting a good list of subscribers but it can be overcome in the following ways:

- Ask research group members if you can add them to your list
- Ask collaborators if you can add them to your list
- Distribute a sign-up link via social media
- Join other peoples' mailing list and ask them to join yours
- Mention your newsletter in events/blogs/speeches/journal articles.

## REPORTS

Reports come in different flavours and colours. They can cover programs, projects, progress, students, research, and administration. They can take various forms from a two-pager to a tome that could rival War and Peace.

However, from the perspective of cut through—the idea that we need to have a message said in the right time, at the right place, and to the right audience—reports should fit their intended purpose. Too often in academia, reports are produced based on what the writer wants to say, rather than for the reader to digest.

For example, an annual report from a scientific or research institute might contain information about the detail of the research undertaken by member researchers. However, if the intended audience or mailing list for the annual report is philanthropists, the public and the government, a large amount of technical data may be off-putting, or difficult to read. Ultimately, the significant and valuable effort you have put in goes to waste.

Other than annual reports, there are few instances where researchers might write a report unsolicited. Yet their knowledge and expertise on a topic lends itself perfectly to the idea of writing on a topic or subject for the purposes of informing a knowledgeable or lay audience. This creates two problems. The first is the lack of practice in writing reports. As highlighted above, this can lead to reports that are not fit for purpose and reports that are too scientific or researchie, when they should engage the reader sufficiently to want to reach out and ask for more.

The second problem is a lack of desire to write a report. Researchers are so busy that an unsolicited report often seems like a waste of time regardless of the actual or perceived potential for success. Even if success could be viewed or measured.

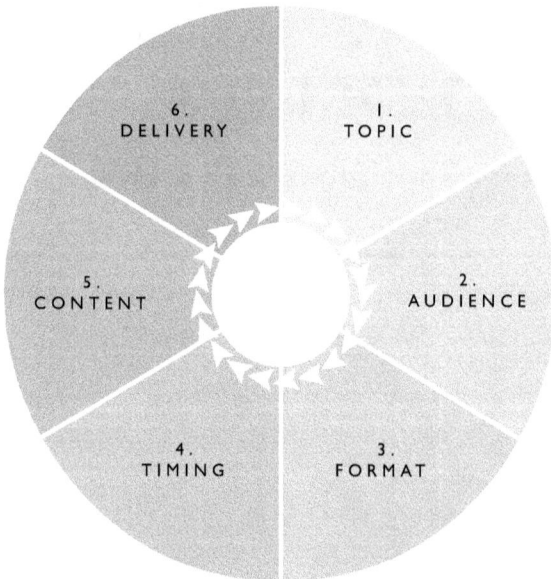

**FIGURE 11:** THE ITERATIVE PROCESS OF CREATING A REPORT

Although I am not advocating writing reports for the sake of it, I am advocating researchers pay closer attention to the idea of self-publishing their ideas in a report-style format, particularly for non-research or non-science audiences.

As mentioned at the start of this section, reports could cover projects, programs (groups of projects) or portfolios (groups of programs). A project might be as small as one experiment or as large as a grant. A program would likely be a grant (especially something as large as a centre of excellence) or several grants. A portfolio could be a large grant or perhaps cover a centre, institute, department, school or faculty. Deciding on what is covered is the first step to writing the report (see figure 11).

This decision might also impact the period covered by the report. There is some advantage to regular reporting particularly to stakeholders or funders of research. As a researcher, regular reporting will help you form good communication habits. Regular reporting will help stakeholders feel connected to the research. Arguably they will be more likely to fund or engage with your current project and/or future projects. The period could be time-based. Annual reports cover a defined 12-month period. Of course, don't write an annual report that is delivered six months late. Rather, have a plan for continual information recording and collecting so report collation is relatively quick and simple. This will reduce the time between the end of the reporting period and the delivery of the report. Of course, you may also report on:

- **Milestones:** achieving a particular result or experiment. This is not to say you need to reach a particular finding, but just that the work is complete. The researcher/research team could define the milestones or they could be described in the funding agreement.

- **Expenditure:** spending a certain amount of money, particularly when the research is funded by a grant.
- **Finding:** achieving a particularly significant finding or result. It could be entirely what you expected or didn't expect. But it might signify a good point to write a report for stakeholders, funders and the public.

The second step is to determine the audience. Funders? End users? Researchers? Policy makers? The more specific you can be the better. Even to the point of having a specific person in mind. Such specificity will allow you to build a report that is far more effective than one intended for all stakeholders. It will also make all other decisions easier: how/why/when will [person's name] want to hear/know about this? As with the other forms of cut through, creating an avatar of the recipient will further help the process of creating a report. For example, the avatar might be:

- 40 years old
- Work fulltime in the public service
- Female
- Have a research background (worked at a university, completed honours but not a PhD)
- Keen to read reports as PDFs, not as paper documents
- Responsible for a small team
- Active on social media.

Once you know the intended audience, all other decisions become easier as you can just pass them through the filter of 'what would our audience want?'

The third step is to determine the format of the report. Format covers all manner of things. It could be if the report is a video, a series of pictures, written words on a screen, hard copy, soft copy, audio etc. Again, your avatar or intended audience will be a big help.

Step four is timing. When or where the recipient would like to receive the report and how long it would take to consume. Seconds? Minutes? Hours? Or would it be read in sections over several days? If this level of detail is not in your avatar's description, be sure to add it in once you are clear on their preferences.

As these decisions are being made, you'll need to move into step five: content. What will you include in the report? All details or a limited number? At the same time as considering what content, it is also useful to consider how easy it is to obtain or generate. My recommendation is to plan in advance. Therefore, if you are creating a written annual report for a centre, you would write short project reports, as you go, which include appropriate images (requiring photos or other pictures be taken/captured at the required resolution). That way, you can combine all of these reports into one at the end of the year, thus allowing rapid publication shortly after the conclusion of the period covered by the report.

You may find the process from topic->audience->format->timing ->content iterative. Furthermore, certain formats will lend themselves better to particular types of content. Similarly, timing might also impact format and content, not to mention the availability of suitable content.

# CHAPTER 9

# IMPLEMENTATION

There are many ways to engage industry and this book has covered but a few. However, it's most important that we cover implementation. That is, turning good ideas or decisions into actions; to implement the ideas you have for engaging or working with industry.

For some, this book might have sparked many ideas, which in turn presents too many options. If that is you, start with one and do it well. Do it better than anyone. If you are reading and are still at a loss for what to do or where to start, try these four steps:

- Plan
- Do
- Review
- Redo

## PLAN

Planning has five steps:

- Identify your audience
- Understand their communication preferences
- Determine the engagement options you will use
- Allocate responsibilities
- Create a schedule.

## IDENTIFY YOUR AUDIENCE

The first step in my process is to know your audience. If you are looking for industry partners, it means knowing who they are and what they want. For most researchers, making a broad list of who would be interested in your work is not too difficult. However, if you don't know who might be interested, here are four places to start looking:

- **Copy others:** Undoubtedly you will know people in your area with industry partners. Look at your peers or competitors and identify their partners. Make a list of those organisations. At this stage, don't filter the list. Just add all non-research partners to it.

- **Grants:** Obviously, any grant with a non-university partner is a potential industry collaborator outside the grant. However, don't limit your thinking to the grants you lead. Look at the grants you are lower investigator on. Not to mention grants you might have held earlier in your career, grants your collaborators might have held and the partners on those activities. Again, no filter, just add them to the list.

- **Key word searches:** What are the key words for your research? Use them in web-based searches and note what organisations appear. Change the keyword to a higher level of abstraction. For example, if you used the name of a protein, now use the name of the signalling pathway it is involved in or the disease in which it is implicated. Perhaps limit the search to a particular location or population. Look through the pages of search results and note down the businesses you find. Don't filter at this point. Note down conferences or groups, not just individual organisations.

- **Social media:** Similar to the keyword search used above, but this time use social media sites such as LinkedIn, Facebook, Instagram and Twitter. It might be necessary to use a #hashtag and to limit the number of words you use. Note down the accounts that use the relevant keywords. There are likely to be many, so it might be worth limiting the list to the top ten only.

Note both business and personal accounts. For the personal accounts look into the business they work for (e.g. by trying to cross reference to Facebook and/or LinkedIn profiles) and note that down too.

Now you should have a list of organisations and/or people who might be potential partners. From there, it's a matter of prioritising which organisation you intend to contact first and for what project or purpose; there are many ways you can do this but I will cover one in detail.

If you are analytical by nature, perhaps putting all organisations into a spreadsheet might be a good place to start. Where relevant, you could include contact details and how you found the entity (e.g. via a collaborator, competitor, social media site, web search etc.). Further columns could be added to the list and each entry scored on different criteria. For example, you might have criteria for:

- **Likelihood of collaborating:** Those who have collaborated with universities or researchers before might score higher on the 'be more likely to work with me' scale than those who have not.
- **Ease of access:** Do you know the organisation or an employee within it? Is contact easy or hard? Do they have an office in your local city? Do they do relevant work in your local city? Do you have their local contact details?
- **Topics covered:** Which topic or keyword led to the inclusion in the list? Is it close to your preferred/perfect topic or a little away from it?
- **Preference:** Do you want to work with the organisation? Are they the type of organisation you could see yourself working with over several months or years? Do they have values that match your own?

Weighting these criteria allows each potential collaborator to be ranked to create a contact priority list. That is, who you will reach out to first, why and how.

It would be best to engage entities identified via social media through the same platform on which you originally identified them. Those organisations you found via a web search might be contacted via their web-based contacted method. You could then create an additional column to acknowledge where contact has been made or what engagement would be preferred.

## UNDERSTAND THEIR COMMUNICATION PREFERENCES

In reviewing and ranking your audience, you will have identified what partners are using what platforms for their current communications (e.g. Twitter, LinkedIn, Facebook). This is the first part of knowing their preferences. The next part is to use your own knowledge about what individuals or organisations like, particularly for those whom you or your peers have encountered in the past.

For those potential partners without a noted preference, you will need to do some investigating to understand the person or organisation further. You could look at their outward-bound communications. For example, do they write blogs or reports or participate in social media? These new insights might cause a re-ranking of the contact list, particularly if a previously short-listed partner clearly prefers communications you are not comfortable delivering.

Update the spreadsheet (or other tracking document) to note what methods of communication will be used for what partners. You can then use this list for the next steps: determining the engagement options and allocating responsibilities.

## DETERMINING ENGAGEMENT OPTIONS

As a lone researcher, or perhaps even as head of a team, it will be a difficult task to engage all your potential partners using all of the identified communications methods. At this point, it is necessary to prioritise the contact list and the contact methods.

If you have put the names into a spreadsheet, you will be able to sort and filter it based on your ideal partner and their preferred communication or engagement method. Doing this will create a list with the best collaborative candidate and your preferred communication as the highest ranked option. This can be the place to start when it comes to creating the engagement plan (see below).

Depending on the number of items in your list and the range of communication options, you will now be able to build the engagement approach for each partner. As part of this process, it might also be possible to create one communication or engagement plan that can be applied to all partners or for several different partners.

Create an avatar for each preferred or actual engagement. This avatar would cover:

- Age
- Gender
- Topic
- Experience
- Desired communication method.

Of course, for some, engagement will require more than one contact point. The spreadsheet might be further modified to include how and when they were contacted, by whom and what topics(s) were covered. You might also add the kinds of topics or words that are most likely to engage them, like a checklist that could be referred to for web, social media or other communications.

Other contact points could include the various methods mentioned in this book. It might also include the conferences they have attend, the networks or groups they belong to, and even the kinds of collaborators with whom they work (research and non-research). In many cases, if you opt to build and maintain such a spreadsheet it might be called a CRM—customer relationship management—tool. There are also free versions of these tools available on the internet to help collate all the relevant information including providing reminders on when to contact potential collaborators.

As you build a list of the things your potential or actual industry partners like, the aim is to meet those requirements as often and as practicably as possible.

## ALLOCATE RESPONSIBILITIES

For people in research teams, groups, departments, schools etc., it will be important to allocate different parts of the engagement process to different people. Some people will be better at different communications approaches like social media versus public speaking versus calling potential clients, where others will have a stronger affinity to a particular partner over others. Naturally, there will be people who are just better suited to doing the research and/or highly scientific communication. Their involvement in the industry engagement process is essential, but only in the research, not in the engagement. There will also be people who would prefer to stay out of the engagement process independent of their ability to do it. In the allocation of responsibilities, it important all of these factors are taken into consideration.

Once allocated, the people involved need to be notified of their role and how it fits within the broader engagement strategy.

# DO

Obviously, Do is the action part of the strategy and has three components.

## IMPLEMENT THE SCHEDULE

Each person within the schedule performs their task(s) as and when they fall due. Information gathered/learned through implementation should be shared with the rest of the team.

As a multi- or single-person team, all information should be recorded in the CRM (or its equivalent) to avoid things like:

- Embarrassing yourself by asking the same thing twice from different people.
- Repeating a task as you're unaware it was not already complete.
- Missing a task you thought you had completed, but had not.
- Forgetting key information (e.g. leave or follow-up dates, or indicative budgets for projects).

## MEET REGULARLY

Daily, weekly, monthly or quarterly is fine. It needs to be regular but also commensurate with how you are engaging industry.

If not already within your implementation schedule, there should be a regular team meeting to cover industry engagement. These meetings should share the information that might be also recorded in the CRM. They should also be used to update others on information that may be easily conveyed in a CRM such as changes to preferences or personnel or if a team member is on leave and they need someone else to step into the breach. These meetings should follow best practice for meetings and have a chairperson, secretary, agendas and minutes. They need not be long.

As necessary, the plans should be updated to reflect new information identified about each partner, team member or engagement method.

### TREAT IT LIKE RESEARCH

Treat the engagement strategy as another research project. Be okay with rejecting or accepting the null hypothesis that you will find a specific industry partner.

Embarking on the engagement strategy can be daunting. It's a bit like writing your first grant and expecting immediate success. However, and similarly to writing your first grant, early successes or disappointments should be taken as learning experiences and not used to determine how your industry engagement activities will progress into the future. Like any experiment, noting down the method and the results will help refine the process and (hopefully) the outcome.

## REVIEW

Treating the engagement attempts like an experiment will help ensure there is sufficient data and/or evidence upon which to review the original plan. The aim of the review is not to apportion blame for success or failure, but rather understand, in a more formal way, what is and is not working for which potential partners. As with any review, it should consist of two parts.

### 1. COMPARE YOUR PLAN TO WHAT YOU ACTUALLY DID

In the first part, review the plan. What did you set out to do? Who was allocated to the different partners and engagement approaches? What did you actually do? What partners were contacted? Did the allocations progress as planned? Did you use all of the intended engagement approaches? What parts of the plan worked? What should be changed in the next plan? What should remain the same? What should be taken out all together and perhaps replaced?

## 2. REVISE

Having established how the plan should be changed, the next step is to update it. Importantly, the improved plan should be shared with relevant participants. Particularly those within and across the research group, department and faculty. There are five areas important to consider as part of the revision.

### Avatar

Has your idea of the perfect partner changed? If so, how? Make the relevant modifications, bearing in mind you might have multiple avatars covering different types of projects or engagement approaches. Or you might need to have multiple avatars or reduce the number you have.

Your approaches might have also unearthed some new engagement methods as more or less effective, not to mention adding new potential partners to the list.

### Communication preferences

The work you've completed will help you understand the communication preferences of you and your partners. Do you prefer a particular social media channel over another? Does someone in the team have a better following than the rest? Does a particular account perform better in particular situations? Note things down and make sure they are taken into account when creating the communication aspects of your engagement strategy. It's also important to consider internal communication. How are you communicating engagement among your team members? Could this be improved? Are the current tools helping or hindering the exchange of information.

### Engagement options

When you started the engagement process, there were likely a different set of engagement options compared to now. How have things changed? Is there a change to the demographics using or accessing the social media channels you prefer? Is there a new social media outlet gaining traction among your target audience? Has the skill set within your group or organisation changed making certain engagement options more or less suitable to your new strategy?

What have you learnt about specific options and partners that make the engagement process different to your original thinking? How should your strategy change to take these new insights into account.

## Responsibilities

If this is the first engagement strategy you've implemented or the first time you've approached it with a scientific mindset, you've probably noted a lot about yourself and your team. In particular, who likes to do what in relation to industry engagement. It's important to review and update these responsibilities and to take this new information into account. This might also be a good time to pair people up and assign different in-house experts to work with others and upskill those who are not as skilled. This also ensures a level of redundancy in the event of catastrophe such as a team member leaving suddenly and/or without warning.

## Schedule

Finally, review the schedule. Was it workable? Did it allow sufficient time for follow-up and/or personalised responses? Was the engagement arranged over a sufficient time? Was it too long? Could you have worked on different days/weeks/months? What activities might be better scheduled for a different time of the day or year? Does a particular kind of social media or engagement event lend itself to a better time of day or year? Does the coming period warrant the schedule going for a longer/shorter time. Will the next engagement strategy be special due to an upcoming milestone or event?

# REDO

Redo is all about implementation of the next engagement strategy, taking into account what you have learned and updated based on the previous engagement strategies.

If this is the third or fourth iteration of your strategy, be mindful that the new schedule and associated implantation should cover everything you have learned to that point—not just the latest attempt. Of course, the schedule should cover the range of activities to perform, who is responsible for each and when they will complete the work.

Similarly, if this is the third or fourth time you are executing your engagement strategy, you may find that fewer or shorter meetings are more effective than the longer more frequent meetings you held in earlier versions. Of course, if you are implementing something new, it might be worth dedicating additional meetings or time within each meeting to cover off those new aspects.

Finally, and most importantly, continue to treat the industry engagement activities as a research experiment. Learn from successes and failures. Change and adapt as you go, and make sure you maintain accurate records so successes can be repeated and failures avoided.

# CONCLUSION

The need for and value in partnering with industry has always been present. However, as PhD training numbers increase; university, state and federal budgets are squeezed; community demand more transparency for how their taxes are spent; and impact from funding is being sought, the demand for researchers to work with industry has never been higher.

Despite these growing demands and pressures, researchers and researchers in training are essentially left to their own devices when it comes to partnering with industry. There is little, if any, support and few guides. Most people believe they must do it all, and all on their own.

Supervisors, having not been through the same pressures themselves, are ill-equipped to provide necessary guidance. For those who have been through the process, the experience is either taken as a hazing ritual to be re-told as a warning to others. Or, it is closely guarded so as not to lose a perceived competitive advantage.

Yet, with thousands of micro businesses (sole traders to ten employees), hundreds of small to medium enterprises (SME, 11–200 employees) and many large businesses (200+ staff) there are countless opportunities for all researchers.

Furthermore, these opportunities are not limited to one particular model or approach. It does not have to be a collaboration; it could be fee for service. It does not have to be a widget; it could be a process. It does not have to be your favourite protein; it could be your favourite cell type. However, the models and case studies put forward are often the ones concerning big businesses buying cures for cancer. It is no wonder Australia sits so lowly on the international scale when it comes to university/industry partnerships and the application of research findings into everyday use(s).

And thus, I leave you with this, a model of why you might work with industry and what might go wrong.

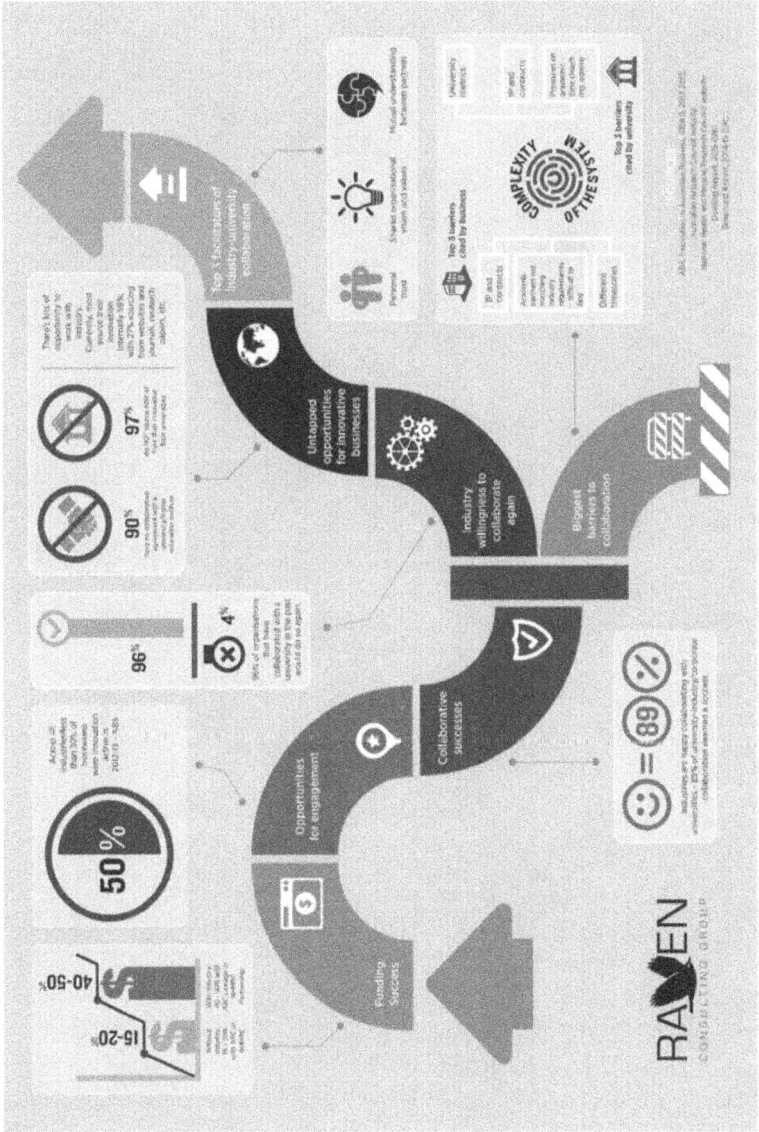

# ABOUT DR RICHARD HUYSMANS

Designs, implements and delivers translational projects that increase collaboration and funding success.

- Published (peer reviewed) author
- PhD graduate (Monash University, Biomedical Science)
- Leader of translational research projects.

Dr Richard Huysmans is driven by the challenge of increasing grant success, building collaboration, engaging industry and obtaining funding. His strategic approach brings universities, research facilitates and organisations together to ensure research has an impact. As a published author combining academic qualifications with sector expertise and research experience, Richard is an insightful and effective professional.

Richard works with leaders in research including Research Managers, Centre and Institute Directors, and Deputy and Pro Vice-Chancellors of Research and Faculty Managers. His recent projects have included building research teams, translating research into practice, engaging industry, and establishing and reviewing research centres.

HOW RICHARD HELPS:

- Keynote Speaker on Translation and Leadership
- Social Media Strategy and Execution for Researchers
- Strategic, Business and Implementation Planning
- Project Management
- Complex Collaborative Proposal Development
- Career Planning and Transition.

## RICHARD'S CLIENTS:

La Trobe University, Monash University, Victorian and Federal Government Departments of Health, Royal District Nursing Service, University of Melbourne, University of Sydney, University of Queensland, Queensland University of Technology.

## GETTING IN TOUCH
## WITH RICHARD:

**Phone:** 0412 606 178

**Email:** richard@DrRichardHuysmans.com

**Website :** www.DrRichardHuysmans.com

**Twitter:** @richardhuysmans

**Instagram:** @drrichardhuysmans

**Facebook group:** facebook.com/ravencg.aus
(Beyond your Phd with Dr Richard Huysmans)

**LinkedIn:** au.linkedin.com/in/richardhuysmans

# ENDNOTES

[1] @PrincessSuperno, 2015. *Twitter.* [Online] Available at: https://twitter.com/search?vertical=default&q=%40princessSuperno [Accessed 17 October 2018].

[2] Although the hashtag is about *science, I prefer research.* There are many fields of endeavour where the focus is research but not necessarily science. However, the term *scientist* accidentally excludes those fields and, therefore, their participants. Examples include politics, our health system (as opposed to health care), religion, society and education.

[3] Of course, the 'publish or perish', career interruption, track-record element means this is entirely impractical within the current system.

[4] Wikipedia, 2011. *File: Diffusion Of Innovation.* [Online] Available at: https://en.wikipedia.org/w/index.php?curid=11484459 [Accessed 17 October 2018].

[5] Faire, J., 2015. The Conversation Hour. [Sound Recording] (ABC Radio) Available at: http://www.abc.net.au/local/audio/2015/08/19/4296369.htm

[6] The Conversation, 2013. *Predicting who will publish or perish as career academics.* [Online] Available at: https://theconversation.com/predicting-who-will-publish-or-perish-as-career-academics-18473 [Accessed 17 October 2018].

[7] Somewhat tongue-in-cheek, many argue a researcher's equivalent hourly rate is almost zero.

[8] At this point, 9–15 years have been invested, and you are still considered a beginner. Compared to almost every other profession, where 3–5 years at university followed by 4–9 years of work will mean you are considered mid-level or even experienced.

[9] Wagner, C. S. et al., 2015. Do Nobel Laureates Create Prize-Winning Networks? An Analysis of Collaborative Research in Physiology or Medicine. *PLOS ONE*, 31 July.

[10] Lewis, T., 2018. *No yolk! Scientists unboil an egg withiut defying physics.* [Online] Available at: https://www.livescience.com/49610-scientists-unboil-egg.html [Accessed 18 October 2018].

[11] Mewburn, D. I. & Maxwell, D. J., 2012. *Write that journal article in 7 days.* [Online] Available at: https://www.slideshare.net/ingermewburn/write-that-journal-article-in-7-days-12742195
[Accessed 18 October 2018].

[12] Unless you're a Nobel laureate, which suggests you produce many solo papers prior to winning a prize.

[13] Bennett, N. & Lemoine, G. J., 2014. What VUCA really means for you. *Harvard Business Review*, Jan-Feb.

[14] Garfield, E., 1996. *What is the primordial reference for the phrase 'publish or perish'?.* [Online] Available at: https://www.the-scientist.com/commentary/what-is-the-primordial-reference-for-the-phrase-publish-or-perish-57976 [Accessed 18 October 2018].

[15,19] Fanelli, D. & lariviere, V., 2016. Reasearchers' individual publication rate has not increased in a century. *PLOS ONE*.

[16] Blair, J., 2012. The publication imperitave. *New Scientist*, 24 April.

[17] Hapsci, 2012. *How many papers should academics publish per year?.* [Online] Available at: http://www.heatherdoran.net/2012/02/how-many-papers-should-academics.html [Accessed 18 October 2018].

[18] Stokstad, E., 2014. The 1%of scientific publishing. *Science Mag*, 11 July.

[20] Anon., n.d. *ResearchGate.* [Online] Available at: https://www.researchgate.net/ [Accessed 06 February 2019].

[21] Wikipedia, n.d. *Unboxing.* [Online] Available at: https://en.wikipedia. org/wiki/Unboxing [Accessed 06 February 2019].

[22] Wright, G., 2015. *The weird and wonderful world of academic Twitter.* [Online] Available at: https://www.timeshighereducation.com/blog/ weird-and-wonderful-world-academic-twitter
[Accessed 18 October 2018].

[23] Lupton, D., 2014. *Feeling better connected: Academics' use of social media,* Canberra: University of Canberra.

[24] Al-Assi, R., n.d. *AndFarAway.* [Online] Available at: www.andfaraway.net [Accessed 18 October 2018].

[25, 26] Department of Education and Training, n.d. [Online] Available at: http://highereducationstatistics.education.gov.au/
[Accessed 18 October 2018].

[27] Like a helicopter parent constantly hovering in or around your work. They are never too far away, ensuring you never fail, but also ensuring you never grow through taking risks and making mistakes from which you might learn.

[28] Atkins, J., 2016. The importance of storytelling in science. *PLOS Ecology Community,* 30 December.

[29] Hillier, A., Kelly, R. P. & Klinger, T., 2016. Narrative style influences citation frequency in climate change science. *PLOS ONE,* 15 December.

[30] Monash University, n.d. *Understanding the human brain.* [Online] Available at: www.cibf.edu.au [Accessed 18 October 2018].

[31] Sensis, 2017. [Online] Available at: https://www.sensis.com.au/about/ our-reports/sensis-social-media-report [Accessed 18 October 2018].

[32] The Great Firewall of China is the prevention of web content making it onto internet-connected computers in China. Facebook, Instagram and Twitter are all blocked by the firewall.

www.ingramcontent.com/pod-product-compliance
Lightning Source LLC
Chambersburg PA
CBHW070407200326
41518CB00011B/2098